FUN·TO·MAKE CRAFTS FOR EVERY DAY

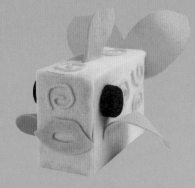

Boyds Mills Press

Editor
Tom Daning

Craft Contributors

Robin Adams
Dorothy Andrisani
Debbie Anilonis
Margaret Ann Aumen
Linda Bloomgren
Debra Boyles
J. B. Boyles
Norma Jean Byrkett
KayLani Campbell
Maureen Casazza
Marie Cecchini
Rosie Centrone
Cory Ann Derr
Nellie deVries
Susan Donaldson
Kent Douglas
Kathy Everett
Mary Fernan

Clara Flammang
Dee Francis
Tanya Turner Fry
Mary Galligan
George Georgeff
Donna M. Graham
Shelley Graham
Leslie Hamilton
Edna Harrington
Emilda Harrington
Joann M. Hart
Susan Hasbrouck
Caroline Hatton
Olive Howie
Helen Jeffries
Tama Kain
Garnett Kooker
Jean Kuhn

Casey Kustra
Barbara Cyr Lind
Dana London
Susan Lucci
Doreen Macklen
Kelli Michaels
Donna Miers
Jerry Mundy
Marianne Myers
Shari O'Rourke
Jenna Osborne
Beatrice Bachrach Perri
James W. Perrin Jr.
Sheila M. Perry
Cheryl Pilgrim
Katherine A. Plaza
Barbara Santucci
Laura Sassi

Becky Sawyer
Bernard Sawyer
Muriel Souza
Andrew J. Smith
Lisa Steele
Cathy Stefanec-Ogren
Catherine Stier
Karen Sweeny-Justice
Emily Sweetme
Sherry Timberman
Sibille Treffkorn
Tammy Vollenweider
Francis Wales
Dava Jo Walker
Cecilia A. Wheeler

Craft Builders

Verlie Hutchens
Jennifer Pereira

Published by Boyds Mills Press, Inc.
A Highlights Company
815 Church Street
Honesdale, Pennsylvania 18431
Printed in China

Publisher Cataloging-in-Publication Data

Fun-to-make crafts for every day / Boyds Mills Press.—1st ed.
[64] p.: col. photos. ; cm.
Includes index.
Summary: Includes step-by-step directions to make decorations, gifts, and
   greeting cards for every day.
ISBN 1-59078-341-7
ISBN 1-59078-366-2 (pbk.)
1. Handicraft — Juvenile literature. I. Title.
745.5 22   TT160.F86 2004

First edition, 2005
Book designed by Janet Moir McCaffrey
The text of this book is set in 11-point New Century Schoolbook.

Visit our Web site at www.boydsmillspress.com

10 9 8 7 6 5 4 3 2 1 hc
10 9 8 7 6 5 4 3 2 1 pb

*I*n these pages you will find more than 140 imaginative craft ideas for every day and special occasions. Gifts, games, toys, decorations, greeting cards—whatever you want to make, it's here. So put on your most stylish paint-splattered smock, roll up your sleeves, and create!

Safety First

Although most crafts in this book are designed for you to make yourself, remember to ask for an adult's help when handling sharp instruments or using the stove.

Follow the Directions— But Add Your Own Flair

To build each craft, follow the steps listed. The directions and the pictures are helpful guides, but they are no substitute for your own imagination. You might figure out a different way to make a Thanksgiving turkey or to decorate a bracelet. Or you might be inspired to make up your own crafts.

Neatness Counts

Before you get crafty, be smart and cover your work area. Old newspapers, brown paper bags, old sheets, or a plastic drop cloth will work. Protect your clothes with an apron, a smock, or a big old shirt. And remember to clean up after you are finished.

Stock Your Craft Workshop

We've included a list of materials to make each craft. Recyclable items such as cardboard tubes, plastic milk bottles, and cereal boxes are needed for many of them. Before you start, check out the items in the materials list for the crafts you plan to make. Ask your parents, friends, and relatives to start saving these things for you, so you will always have a supply on hand. If you don't have the exact item listed, something else may work just as well. Make sure you clean and dry the recyclables before using them. Also, good crafters usually keep some supplies handy—such as scissors, crayons, markers, craft glue, tape, pens, pencils, paint, a hole punch, and a stapler. Because these are used so frequently, we don't include them in the list of materials.

Have Fun!

Personalized Stone

flat stone ● glaze or clear nail polish

1. Using a light color, paint a circle in the middle of a flat stone.
2. When it's dry, paint your initial in it with a dark color.
3. Paint your own design around the circle.
4. When dry, coat your stone with a glaze or clear nail polish.

Bumble Bee Pal

2½-inch plastic-foam ball ● felt ●
2-inch, 1-inch, and ¼-inch black pompoms
● wiggle eyes

1. Cut a bit off the bottom of a 2½-inch plastic-foam ball so it doesn't roll, and glue black felt to the flat part.
2. Glue on alternating ½-inch-wide felt strips of yellow and black until the ball is covered.
3. Glue on a 2-inch black pompom for the head and 1-inch pompoms for feet.
4. Glue on wiggle eyes, a ¼-inch pompom for the nose, a red felt mouth, and two black felt antennae.
5. Roll a small cone from black felt and glue it on for a stinger. Cut two wings from white felt and glue them on the bee's back.

St. Pat's Hat Game

green paper ● cardboard oatmeal container

1. Make a leprechaun hat by gluing green paper around an oatmeal container and decorating it. (Discard the lid.)
2. Cut out a large cardboard circle. Glue on green paper.
3. Glue the bottom of the container to the middle of the circle. Decorate with paper clovers and flowers.
4. Assign points to the hat and brim. Toss coins at the hat, then add up your score. Between games, use it as a centerpiece.

Patriotic Pencil Holder

paper ● frozen-juice container

1. Glue blue paper around the outside of a frozen-juice container.
2. Glue a 3-inch-wide strip of white paper around the base of the container.
3. Glue three ½-inch-wide strips of red paper onto the white strip, spacing them ½ inch apart.
4. Cut white stars from paper, and glue them around the container.

The Chenille Family

chenille sticks ● fabric ● ribbon or yarn ● paper

1. Cut three 6-inch-long pieces of chenille stick. Fold back ½ inch at each end of the pieces to get rid of any sharp ends.
2. To make the head and arms, make a loop the size of a dime in the center of one chenille piece. Twist the bottom of the loop twice. Bend the folded ends up to make hands.
3. For the legs and body, twist together 1 inch of the other two pieces of chenille stick, starting halfway up. Twist each short end around a "shoulder." Bend up the other ends to make feet.
4. Cut strips of fabric scraps for clothes. Starting and finishing at the waist of the doll, wrap the strips around the body. Tie a piece of ribbon, yarn, or fabric around the waist to hold the ends in place.
5. Make a hat from fabric or paper.
6. Vary the length of the chenille-stick pieces to make smaller or larger dolls.

Keys, Please!

corrugated cardboard ● felt ● chenille stick ● yarn

1. Cut a 3-inch-wide rectangle from corrugated cardboard. (The length depends on how big a key holder you want to make.)
2. Glue felt to one side of the cardboard.
3. With a pencil, lightly mark off where you want the key hangers to be (every few inches down the center of the felt).
4. Poke a hole through the cardboard at one of the pencil marks. Fold a 6-inch piece of chenille stick in half and twist it together from the folded end to within 1 inch of the ends. Push the ends through the hole to the back of the key holder. Spread the ends apart and tape them to the cardboard. Repeat for each pencil mark.
5. To hang the key holder, glue a yarn loop to the back. Then glue a piece of felt on the back to cover the ends of the chenille sticks and the yarn loop. Let it dry. Glue on felt decorations.

Golf-Dad Trophy

shoe box ● paper ● plastic bottle caps ● clay ● golf tees ● plastic-foam balls or table-tennis balls

1. Cover a shoe box and its lid with green paper.
2. Fill three small plastic bottle caps with green clay. Glue the flat part of each to the top of the box.
3. Paint a greeting (like "Number 1" or "You're Tee-rific!") on the box, or cut the words from paper and glue them on.
4. Press the pointed end of a golf tee into the clay in each cap.
5. Use paint or markers to put the letters D A D (or P O P) on three 1½-inch plastic-foam balls or table-tennis balls, one letter on each.
6. Glue the balls onto the tees to spell out "DAD" or "POP." Give the trophy box to your father for Father's Day.

Cozy Cradle

cardboard oatmeal container ● masking tape ● paper or gift wrap ● lightweight cardboard ● fabric

1. Remove the lid of an empty cardboard oatmeal container. Cut a large, curved, rectangular piece from the container, as shown.

Earth Day Medallion

pods, shells, beans, and seeds ● circle of corrugated cardboard ● string ● clear packing tape

1. Use natural materials like pods or shells, or dried things from your cupboard like beans and seeds, to create a design on a cardboard circle, rearranging to try different looks.
2. When you are satisfied with your design, glue it in place.
3. Knot each end of an 8-inch piece of string. Use clear packing tape to secure the string to the back of the medallion for hanging.

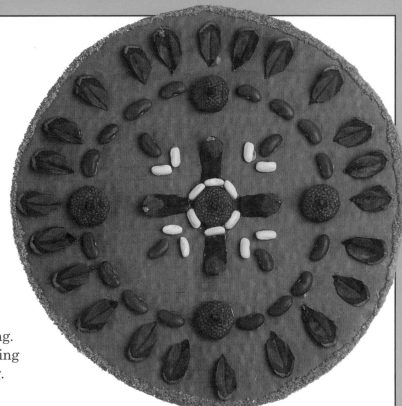

2. Replace the lid and attach it with masking tape or glue.
3. Cover the outside of the box with paper or gift wrap. Trim the edges with masking tape. Color the tape.
4. If you want to add rockers to the cradle, cut two large crescent shapes from lightweight cardboard and paint them. Cut two slits in the bottom of the cradle, and slide the crescents into the slits.
5. Line the inside of the cradle with a fabric scrap to make a soft bed for a small doll or stuffed animal.

Box Camera

cardboard tube ● juice box ● plastic wrap ● aluminum foil ● toothpaste cap ● fabric

1. Stand a cardboard tube in the middle of the front of an empty juice box. Trace around it. Cut out the circle, making a hole.
2. To make a viewfinder, cut out a small rectangle just above the hole and a matching rectangle in the back. Cover the holes with pieces of clear plastic wrap, taped in place.
3. To make the camera lens, cut a 2-inch-long section of the cardboard tube. Glue it into the hole.
4. Paint the box or cover it with aluminum foil.
5. Glue on a toothpaste cap for a shutter button.
6. Glue a long strip of fabric to the sides of the camera for a carrying strap.

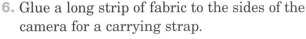
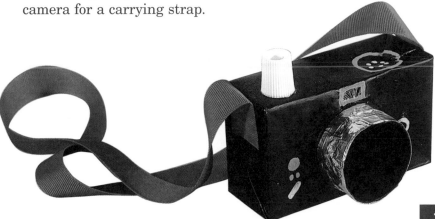

Bulbous Bee

small light bulb ● toothpick ● paper ● string

1. Paint a small light bulb yellow. When dry, paint four black stripes around the bulb. Paint the base and tip of the bulb black. Use a toothpick and white paint to make two eyes on the front of the base.
2. Draw two oval wings on white paper. Draw veins on the wings with a marker and cut the wings out. Overlap the wings slightly and glue them to the back of the bulb.
3. Tie a string around the base of the bulb to hang.

Crafty Gobblers

plastic-foam balls ● craft sticks ● yarn ● chenille sticks ● felt ● drinking straws

1. To make the body, cut a 3-inch plastic-foam ball in half and paint one of the halves brown. For the head, paint a 2-inch plastic-foam ball brown. Let dry.
2. Poke 1 inch of a craft stick into the center of the head. Poke 1 inch of the other end of the stick straight down into the curved side of the body, about 1 inch away from the cut edge.
3. Put glue on the craft stick and wrap it with yarn until it is covered.
4. To make the beak, cut a 3-inch-long piece of yellow chenille stick. Fold it in half. Push the folded end into the face.

"Egg"-cellent Octopus Pencil Holder

plastic-foam egg ● beads ● chenille sticks ● wiggle eyes

1. Cut the end off a plastic-foam egg so that it can sit flat. Poke a hole all the way through the egg with a pencil. Remove the pencil.
2. Paint the egg.
3. Thread one bead onto a chenille stick and bend the end around the bead to secure. From the other end, add three more beads onto the leg. Repeat until you have eight legs.
4. Poke the legs into the egg, spacing them evenly all around. Bend the legs out.
5. Glue on wiggle eyes.

5. Glue on felt eyes. Cut a strip of red felt. Glue it on between the eyes and over the beak to make a wattle.
6. Poke holes in the body with a pencil. Put glue in each hole and insert cut drinking straws. Or poke the holes with painted craft sticks, and glue them into the holes.

Piggy Patriot

felt ● large plastic juice bottle and lid ● plastic bottle caps ● buttons ● paper

1. Cut blue felt to cover the barrel of a large plastic juice bottle. Glue it in place so the ends meet. Add red and white felt stripes.

2. Glue the tops of four small plastic bottle caps to the bottle, two to each side of the felt seam, to make legs.
3. Glue on felt ears. To make eyelashes and eyes, glue on felt stars. Add buttons.
4. Cut a felt tail. Stiffen by laying it flat and covering it with a thin layer of glue. Let dry. Then glue it to the bottle.
5. Decorate the pig with stars cut from paper or felt. Put two stars on the top of the bottle lid to make the snout.

Hanging Flowers

cardboard tube ● cardboard ● ribbon ● flowers ● wet tissue ● aluminum foil

1. Select a cardboard tube. Cut out a cardboard circle that is a little wider than the tube. Glue it on one end. Decorate the tube.
2. Near the end opposite the base, punch a hole in each side of the tube. Tie on ribbon as a hanger.
3. With an adult's permission, pick some flowers. Wrap their stems in wet tissue and cover with aluminum foil. Place the stems in the tube. (If using artificial flowers, place them directly in the tube.)
4. Hang the arrangement on a doorknob, a nail, or anywhere that your mom can enjoy it.

Sparkly Mask

paper ● lightweight cardboard ● aluminum foil ● sequins
● feathers ● glitter ● ribbons ● wooden dowel

1. Hold a piece of paper over your eyes and have an adult mark where your eyes are with a crayon. Remove the paper from your face. Cut out an oval at each eye mark.
2. Place the pattern in the middle of a 10-inch piece of lightweight cardboard and trace the ovals. Remove the pattern. Draw a mask shape around the ovals. Cut the mask and eyeholes from the cardboard.
3. Trace the mask and eyeholes onto aluminum foil. Cut out the foil and glue it to the mask.
4. Decorate the mask with sequins, paper cutouts, feathers, glitter, or ribbon.
5. Tape a thin wooden dowel to one side of the mask at the back, and use the dowel to hold the mask up to your face.

Mini Cuckoo Clock

construction paper ● macaroni-and-cheese box ● white paper
● metal fastener

1. Cut and glue brown construction paper onto a macaroni-and-cheese box. After it dries, cut a door. Snip only three sides, so it can open and close.
2. Glue a purple paper rectangle onto the door. Then cut a slightly smaller brown rectangle from paper. Snip a narrow slit for the doorknob. To make the knob, slip a folded scrap of purple paper through the slit. Tape it in the back. Glue the brown rectangle onto the purple one.
3. For the clock face, glue on a circle of white paper. When dry, add numbers, poke a hole in the middle, and attach a metal fastener to two black hands and the face.
4. Cut a 24-inch-by-1-inch strip of construction paper. Fold it accordion style. Draw a small cuckoo bird onto construction paper. Glue the bird to one end of the folded strip. Tape the other end inside the clock. Close the door.
5. Glue on a gray paper mouse and add your final details. To make your bird pop out, open the door.

Porthole Scene

clear plastic lid ● construction paper ● rope
● masking tape ● twine

1. For the porthole, use a clear round plastic lid from a take-out container or a plastic top from a ready-made pie crust.
2. From construction paper, cut out a ship, water, and other details to make a scene that fits in the porthole. Glue the scene together, but don't glue it in the porthole.
3. Add a few dots of glue to the front of the scene, and place it facedown on the inside of the porthole.
4. Measure a piece of rope to fit around the outside edge. Glue it in place and let dry.
5. On the back, use masking tape to add a twine hanger.

Tiny Turtle

green chenille stick ● dark green beads
● tiny wiggle eyes

1. Fold a green chenille stick in half. Thread one bead onto each half, leaving about ½ inch of chenille stick for the head.
2. Bend a small part of each chenille-stick half to make the front legs. Add two beads to each half. Repeat to form the back legs. Add one more bead to each half. Twist the ends together to make the tail. Trim off the excess with scissors.
3. Pinch the legs, and form the shape of a turtle. Glue on wiggle eyes. Let dry.

Magnetic Paper-Clip Holder

small cardboard box ● pebbles ●
black construction paper ● magnetic sheet

1. Fill a small cardboard box with pebbles to give it weight. Tape the ends of the box closed. Use tape and black construction paper to cover the box.
2. Measure and cut six pieces from a magnetic sheet to fit each side of the box. Glue the magnetic-sheet pieces to the sides and ends of the box.

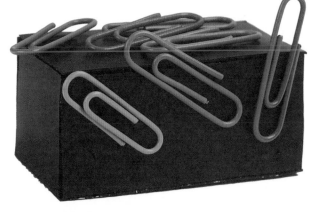

Signs of Love

paper ● poster board ● string

Many people who are deaf or hard of hearing use sign language to communicate. The sign language symbol for "I Love You," which is used in this craft, combines the letters, I, L, and Y together into one symbol.

1. Trace around one of your hands on paper. Cut out the tracing.
2. Cut out a poster-board heart larger than the traced paper hand. Cut out another heart from poster board about an inch larger all around than the first. Glue the smaller heart to the larger one.
3. Glue the hand to the poster board, leaving the ring finger and middle finger unglued.
4. Curl or bend the two unglued fingers forward, and glue them to the palm of the paper hand.
5. Write "I Love You" on the poster board. Attach string to hang up the craft, or give it to someone special as a Valentine's Day Card.

Bedside Book Caddy

felt ● fabric paint ● cardboard

1. Cut out an 8½-inch-square piece of felt. Place it on top of an 8½-inch-by-11½-inch piece of felt, matching the bottom corners.
2. Fold down a 1-inch section on the top piece, and glue it in place. To form a pocket, stitch or glue the side and bottom edges of both pieces where they meet.
3. Add details and a message with fabric paint. Cut out a moon and some stars from felt. Glue them on.
4. Glue the top edge of your caddy to one end of a large cardboard rectangle. Let dry.
5. Slide the cardboard between the mattress and box spring on your bed.

Liberty Bird

cardboard tube ● construction paper
● paper plate

1. To make the body, paint a short cardboard tube. Cut one end to form a V shape in the front and back.
2. Cut the eagle's head from white construction paper. Use markers or crayons to add the details. Glue the head onto the uncut end of the tube.
3. Cut large wings from dark brown construction paper. Glue them to the back of the body.
4. Glue paper legs and talons to the body.
5. To make tail feathers, use half of a paper plate. Roll it into a cone shape and tape it together on the inside and outside. Then place the eagle's body on top of the cone and stand the eagle upright.

Nesting Bears

cardboard tubes
● paper

1. Collect three 4½-inch-long cardboard tubes. Set aside one for the large bear.
2. For the medium bear, cut off 1 inch from the top of a tube. Then cut the tube open lengthwise. Cut off an inch-wide strip from the side of the tube, and tape the edges back together.
3. For the small bear, cut off 2 inches from the top of a tube. Then cut the tube open lengthwise. Cut off a 2-inch-wide strip from the side, and tape the edges back together.
4. Create a head, body, legs, and feet from paper. Glue them on. Add details with markers.

Fancy Fish

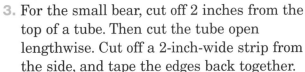

cookie box ● felt ● plastic bottle caps ● yarn

1. Cover a cookie box with felt.
2. Cut out fins, a tail, and lips from a contrasting color of felt and glue the pieces in place.
3. Cover the two bottle caps with black felt and glue them on for eyes.
4. Make designs on the body of your fish by drawing them on with glue and then pressing pieces of yarn into the designs.

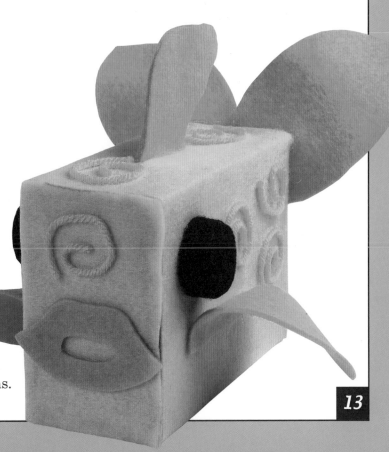

Tabletop Billiards

felt ● drinking straw ● unsharpened pencils ● marbles

1. Cut a piece of felt into three 9-inch-by-4-inch sections. Glue the three sections one on top of the other. Let dry.
2. Cut the three-layer felt into four ¾-inch-wide strips. Cut two of the strips in half, and trim the other two strips so that each is 7 inches long. Trim all the ends to 45-degree angles.
3. Glue the strips around the edges of a piece of 9-inch-by-12-inch felt to form the four corners and two side holes of a pool table.
4. Fold and tape a drinking straw into a triangle with 3½-inch sides for a ball rack.
5. To play, use unsharpened pencils as cues, marbles as balls, and a different-colored marble as a cue ball.

Tubular Critter

cardboard tube ● paper

1. Paint a small cardboard tube.
2. Cut paper features for whatever critter you'd like to make. Glue them to the tube. Add other features with markers.
3. Set the critter on your shelf, or use it as a finger puppet.

Scrap-Fabric Place Cards

poster board ● fabric ● pinking shears ● ribbon or lace scraps

1. For each place card, cut a 3-inch square from poster board.
2. Glue a 3-inch square of fabric over the poster board. Let dry.
3. Trim the edges of the card with scissors or pinking shears.
4. Fold the cards in half. Print a name on the card, using a marker that won't spread on the fabric.
5. Decorate around the card with ribbon or lace scraps.

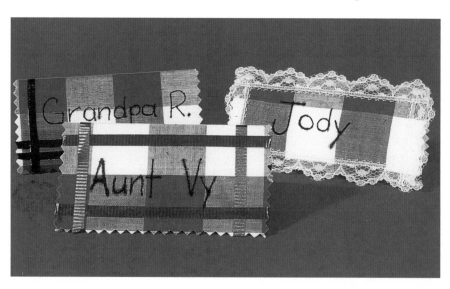

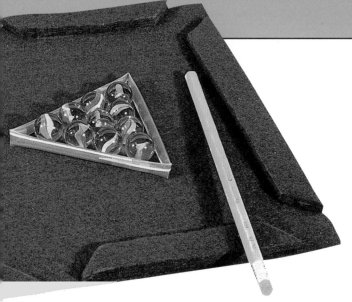

Fan Card

construction paper ● heart-shaped paper doilies ● ribbon ● craft stick

1. Draw and cut out two heart shapes from construction paper. Glue a heart-shaped paper doily to each paper heart.
2. Cut two lengths of ribbon. Cut out four small hearts from construction paper. Using a different color, cut four more that are slightly smaller. Glue a ribbon in between a small heart and a smaller heart, as shown.
3. Color a craft stick with red marker. Tape the end of the craft stick to the construction-paper side of one of the doily hearts. Tape the ribbon ends to the same heart on either side of the craft stick. Glue the remaining doily heart to your first heart, covering the ends of the craft stick and ribbon.
4. Draw and cut a smaller paper heart. Write the message "You're FANtastic" on this heart. Glue to the front of the card.

Buddy Bookworm

chenille sticks ● wiggle eyes

1. Hold two chenille sticks together so that 2 inches of the sticks overlap. Twist the overlapped parts together.
2. Coil the chenille stick tightly around a pencil. Then pull the pencil out, leaving the chenille stick coiled to form an inchworm.
3. Bend another chenille stick in half. Twist an inch at each end of the folded chenille stick around an end of the inchworm.
4. Glue wiggle eyes to one end of the inchworm.
5. Push up the middle of the coiled inchworm.
6. Use the bent chenille stick to mark your page in a book. Your inchworm will rest on the top of the page.

Ladybug Locket

walnut shell ● felt ● wiggle eyes ● photo ● ribbon

1. Carefully crack a walnut and remove the nut. Paint one half of the shell red. Let dry.
2. Cut and glue spots and a head from black felt. Add two wiggle eyes.
3. Find a small photo of someone special. Using your ladybug shell, trace around the part of the photo you want to keep. Cut it out.
4. Cut a strand of ribbon long enough to make a necklace. Tie the ends in a knot.
5. Apply glue and press the knotted end to the inside of the shell. Then add glue around the rim. Press your photo into the glue. Let dry.

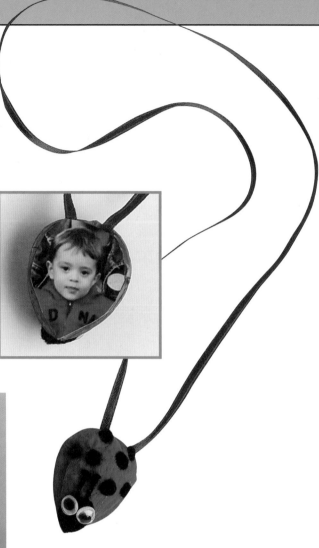

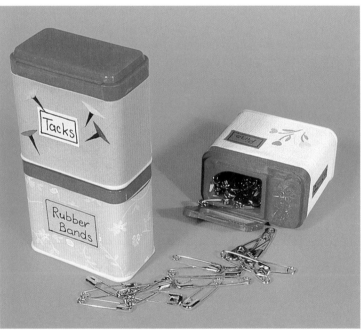

Catch-All Boxes

spice boxes ● self-adhesive shelving paper ● paper

1. Cover empty spice boxes with scraps of self-adhesive paper.
2. Make and glue on a paper label to tell what item is stored in the box.
3. Stack the filled boxes on your desk or shelf.

Heart-Tac-Toe

poster board ● construction paper ● envelope

1. Cut a large heart, about 10 inches across, from poster board and paint it.
2. To make the lines on the game board, cut four strips of poster board and paint them black. When dry, glue them to the board.
3. For kisses, cut five small X shapes from one color of construction paper. For hugs, cut five small O shapes from another color.
4. Write a greeting on the back of the game board. Put the hugs and kisses in an envelope and attach it to the game board with a paper clip. Give the game to a relative or friend for Valentine's Day.

Pompom Piggy

Four ½-inch wooden spools ● large and small pink pompoms ● tiny wiggle eyes ● pink button ● pink chenille stick

1. Paint four spools with pink paint. Let dry completely. Bunch the spools together for the feet. Put a generous amount of glue on the tops of the spools and press the large pompom firmly down on top of them.
2. Glue on a pompom for the head. Glue on wiggle eyes and a button nose.
3. Cut a ½-inch piece of chenille stick. Curl it and glue it on for a tail. Cut two tiny pieces of chenille stick and fold each in half for ears. Glue them onto the head.

Nuts About Turkey

felt ● paper cup ● wooden ice-cream spoon ● yarn

1. Cut turkey wings and tail feathers from felt.
2. Glue them in place on an upright paper cup.
3. Trace around a wooden ice-cream spoon on felt to make a head and neck. Cut out the shape. Add features cut from felt.
4. Glue the head and neck shape to the spoon, then glue the spoon to the cup with the felt facing out. Hold it in place with a clothespin or rubber band until it dries. Add a wattle made of yarn.
5. When dry, fill the cup with nuts or raisins.

Foam Feathered Friends

plastic-foam tray ● metal fastener ●
small plastic container ● twig

1. Cut the shape of a bird from a plastic-foam tray. Cut two wings from the tray.
2. Fasten the wings to the body with a metal fastener. Draw an eye with a pen.
3. Poke a hole in the bottom of a small plastic container, such as a pudding cup.
4. Tape one end of a twig to the back of the bird. Place the container upside down on the table. Push the other end of the twig into the hole.
5. Make an arrangement of different-colored birds on twigs of different lengths.

"Fan"-ciful Card

craft sticks ● greeting card ● yarn

1. Lay two craft sticks side by side. Cover the line between them with glue, and press another craft stick on top of the glue. Wipe away the excess glue and let dry.
2. Open a greeting card. Spread a thin layer of glue all over the inside of the card. Place the upper half of the glued-together craft sticks on the opened card, as shown, to make the handle of the fan. Press the card closed. Let dry.
3. Use a hole punch to make holes around the edges.
4. Beginning close to the handle, weave yarn through the holes. Tie a bow at the end. Use the fan to make a cool breeze.

Puzzle Sticks

craft sticks

1. Lay twelve craft sticks side by side. Line the ends up evenly. Tape the sticks to keep them lined up, then number them from one to twelve. Flip the sticks over.
2. Use a pencil to sketch a picture on the untaped side. Color the picture with markers. Remove the tape from the back.
3. Mix up the sticks, then try to put them back together. You can make a more difficult puzzle by using more sticks.

Sweetheart Bracelet

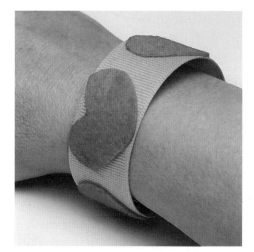

plastic soda bottle ● ribbon ● red felt

1. Cut a ring of plastic from a plastic soda bottle. Snip the ring to form a bracelet. Glue ribbon over the outside of the bracelet.
2. Cut three heart shapes from red felt. Glue the hearts to the ribbon side of the bracelet, spacing them evenly.
3. Give the bracelet to a special friend on Valentine's Day or to your mom on Mother's Day.

Froggy Doorstop

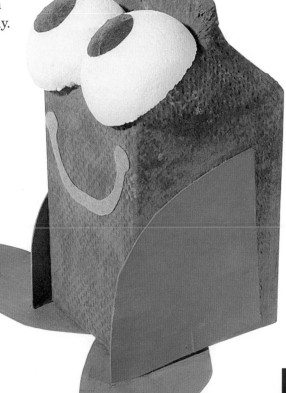

small milk carton ● stones ● paper towels ● cardboard ● plastic-foam ball ● construction paper

1. Fill a small empty milk carton with stones. Tape it shut. Cover it with a layer of paper towels glued in place.
2. Cut legs and feet from cardboard. Glue them to the box. Let dry.
3. Paint the frog green.
4. Cut a small plastic-foam ball in half. Glue the halves to the box for eyes. Cut a construction-paper mouth and pupils for the eyes. Glue them in place.

Turkey Toss

construction paper ● cardboard egg carton
● cardboard ● candy corn

1. Draw and cut out a circle of tan construction paper for the turkey body. Draw and cut out a turkey head and neck shape from the same paper. Glue the shape to the body. Add eyes with marker.
2. Draw and cut out turkey feet from orange paper, a wattle from red paper, and a small diamond shape from yellow paper. Glue the feet to the bottom of the turkey and the wattle to the head. Fold the diamond shape in half to form the turkey's beak. Glue one side of it next to the wattle. The turkey's beak should open.
3. Cut five cups from a cardboard egg carton. Paint them in bright fall colors for the turkey's tail. Cut out five paper circles to fit inside the cups. Write point numbers on the circles, and glue one circle into each cup.
4. Cut a square of cardboard that will hold the turkey and its tail. Cover the cardboard with paper and tape it on the back. Glue the turkey to the cardboard. Arrange the cups around the top of the turkey for the tail. Glue them in place.
5. To play, each player takes a turn tossing five pieces of candy corn at the turkey's tail. Each player's score is the total number of points earned in the five tosses. The player with the highest score wins that round.

Paper Dress-Up Doll

poster board ● yarn ● gift wrap

1. On poster board, draw two identical doll shapes, or trace a gingerbread cookie cutter twice. Cut out the figures and glue them together.
2. Use markers to draw on a face and shoes.
3. Glue on yarn hair. Or, to make hair as shown in the photo, cut twenty pieces of yarn, each about 2½ inches long. Punch ten holes around the edge of the head. Fold two pieces of yarn in half. Insert the folded ends halfway through the hole to make a loop. Pass the cut ends of the yarn pieces over the poster board and push them through the loop. Pull the ends tightly to secure. Repeat for each hole, using two pieces of yarn for each.

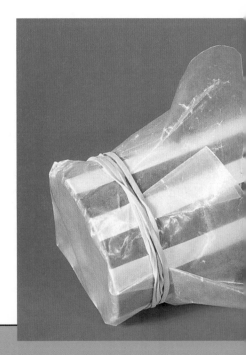

Flowers by the Handful

paper ● construction paper ● button ● chenille sticks ● berry basket ● ribbon

1. Trace the outline of your hand (with the fingers together) and wrist on paper. Cut it out.
2. Use a marker to add details. Cut out a cuff from construction paper and glue it to the wrist. Glue on a button.
3. Cut flowers and leaves from paper. Tape them to chenille-stick stems or to the top edge of a piece cut from a plastic berry basket. Weave ribbon through the holes in the basket piece, and attach a handle made from a chenille stick.
4. Decorate the flowers with ribbon or with a Mother's Day greeting glued in place.
5. Loosely fold the fingers over the stems or basket handle. Glue the fingers to the palm of the hand.

4. Cut doll clothes from gift wrap, using the doll as a guide. Add tabs at the shoulders and waist of the clothes before you cut them out.
5. To dress the doll, fold the tabs over the shoulders and around the waist.

Star-Spangled "Kazoo"

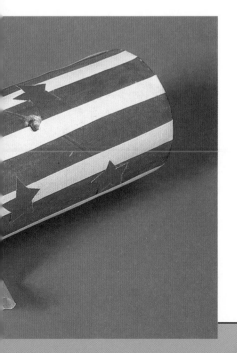

cardboard tube ● paint or paper ● waxed paper ● rubber band

1. Decorate a short cardboard tube with paint or paper. Let it dry.
2. Cut a 4-inch square of waxed paper. Cover one end of the cardboard tube with it, and use a rubber band to hold it in place.
3. Make two or three pencil marks along the top of the tube. Poke a hole in the tube at each mark.
4. Hum into the open end of the tube, and play the "kazoo" by covering and uncovering the holes with your fingers.

Hand-Printed T-Shirt

T-shirt ● cardboard ● clothespins ● newspaper ● rag ● towel ● fabric paint

1. Wash and dry the T-shirt to remove the sizing. Then place a large piece of cardboard inside the shirt to keep the paint from seeping through to the back. Use clothespins to hold the cardboard in place.
2. Use a floor as your work surface. Cover it with layers of newspaper. Have a damp rag and an old towel handy to wipe your hands between colors. Place the T-shirt on the newspapers.
3. To make the tulips and butterfly, put a glob of fabric paint into your palm. Smear it over your foot or your hand (except your thumb) and press it against the shirt. Lift it straight off to prevent smudging. Clean your hand or foot.

4. To make bees, ladybugs, and the body of the butterfly, use a small amount of paint on your thumb to make thumbprints. Draw smaller details, such as words, leaves, stems, and the bees' wings, with a fingertip or a paintbrush.
5. Wash your hands and feet with soap and water. Let the shirt dry completely, following the directions on the paint tubes.

Frog Prince

large juice can ● felt ● cardboard

1. Cover the sides and top of a large juice can with green felt.
2. Cut out two hind legs and two front legs from cardboard, cover them with green felt, and glue them in place.
3. Cut out eyes and a big smile from felt and glue them on.
4. Cut out a crown from cardboard, cover both sides with yellow felt, and form it into a ring.
5. Glue the crown to the head.

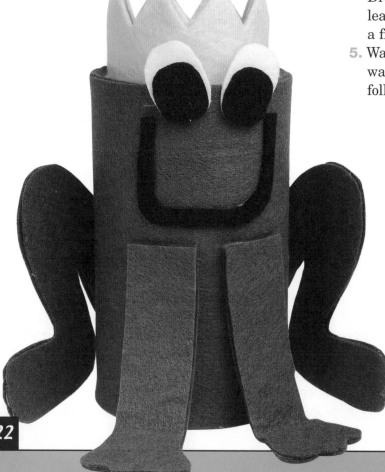

A Grand Old Collage

heavy paper ● old catalog or magazine ● yarn

1. Draw a flag on heavy paper.
2. Cut red, white, and blue areas from pictures in an old catalog or magazine.
3. Cut small sections of each color, and glue them to the flag to make the stripes and the field of blue.
4. Use a hole punch to make thirteen white dots. Glue them in a circle on the blue field. To hang the flag, tape yarn to the back.

Fine Felt Flower

Leaves

Outer petals

Center of flower

felt ● safety pin ● drinking straw

1. From felt, cut the shapes shown at left: a four-pointed star to make the leaves, a clover shape for the outer petals of the flower, and a dog-bone shape for the center.
2. Cut a small slit in the center of the leaf and petal pieces so that the ends of the slits point in the directions shown. Put the petal piece on top of the leaves so that the slits line up.
3. Fold the bone shape in half so the ends meet. Pull the fold through the slits in the other two pieces.
4. To make a pin, attach a safety pin to the fold behind the flower. To make a long-stemmed flower, glue a drinking straw inside the loop that is made by the fold at the back of the flower.

Caterpillar Crawler

chenille sticks ● wiggle eyes ● fishing line

1. Coil a chenille stick (or two chenille sticks, side by side) tightly around a pencil.
2. Slide the coiled chenille stick from the pencil. Carefully tuck all of the sharp ends into the coil.
3. Glue two small wiggle eyes to an end of the chenille stick.
4. Tie one end of a piece of fishing line (1 to 1½ feet long) to the coil close behind the eyes. Tie a loose loop in the other end. Put your finger through the loop and "teach" your pet some commands, such as "come," "stay," and "roll over."

Doll Pin

lightweight cardboard ● yarn ● embroidery floss ● pompoms ● beads ● fabric ● ribbon ● buttons ● safety pin

1. Draw a small doll shape on lightweight cardboard. Cut it out.
2. Paint on a face, hands, and legs, or decorate with markers. Let dry. Then make hair by gluing on yarn, embroidery floss, small pompoms, or beads.
3. Cut fabric clothes and shoe shapes, and glue them to the doll. Trim with ribbon, beads, or small buttons. Let dry.
4. Glue a safety pin to the back of the doll. Let dry.

Lid Game

jar lid ● lightweight cardboard ● paper ● beads ● clear plastic disposable food container

1. Trace around a shallow jar lid twice onto lightweight cardboard and once onto a piece of paper. Cut out the circles and trim them to fit inside the lid.
2. Glue the paper circle inside the lid for the base.
3. Glue the cardboard circles to each other. When the glue has dried, draw a picture on one side of the cardboard with markers or colored pencils. The picture should have several small circles in

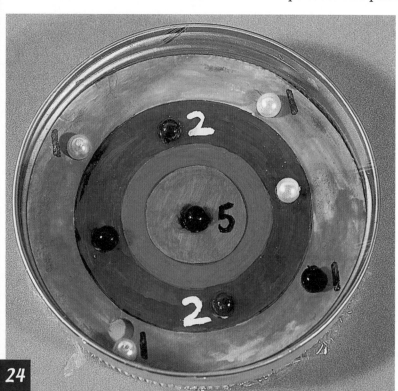

the scene. For example, you might draw a clown juggling balls, an orange tree, or a target with points by each circle.
4. Use a hole punch to make holes in place of the small circles you have drawn.
5. Glue the cardboard inside the lid on top of the paper, with the picture facing up.
6. Put small beads in the lid, one for each hole.
7. Trace around the jar lid onto a clear plastic disposable food container, cut out the circle, and glue it to the rim of the lid.
8. Play the game by wiggling the lid to put all the beads in the holes.

Garden-Patch Markers

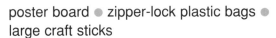

poster board ● zipper-lock plastic bags ● large craft sticks

1. For each marker, cut a piece of poster board about 6 inches wide and 3 inches high.
2. Lightly pencil in a garden-patch name.
3. Put some poster paint on a paper plate. Press your thumb or finger into the paint and then onto the marker. Use your prints to make bugs out of the round-shaped letters and to create fingerprint vegetables. When the paint dries, use black marker to trace over your letters and add details to your bugs and vegetables.
4. Seal your garden markers in zipper-lock plastic bags. For stakes, tape large craft sticks to the back. Then place them in your garden.

Aliens from Planet Pompom

heavy cardboard ● yarn ● felt ● wooden spool ● hairpin ● beads

1. Cut a small rectangle from heavy cardboard. (We used a 2-inch-by-3-inch piece for the larger pompom and a ¾-inch-by-3-inch piece for the smaller one.)
2. Cut a piece of yarn about 7 inches long. Loosely tape it to the length of the cardboard piece.
3. Wrap yarn around the width of the cardboard and over the 7-inch piece of yarn. (We wrapped the large pompom ninety times and the short one forty times.)
4. Bend the cardboard. Slide off the yarn. Wrap the 7-inch piece of yarn tightly around the middle of the loops and tie a knot. Cut through the loops of yarn directly opposite the knot.
5. Fluff out the ends of the yarn, making a ball. Trim the ends.
6. Cut feet from felt. Glue them to the pompom, or glue both pompom and feet to a decorated wooden spool.
7. Glue a bent hairpin to the pompom to make antennae. Glue beads to the ends of the hairpin, if desired. Add bead eyes.

Turkey-Plate Special

paper plate ● brown paper bag ● paper clip or string

1. Use a pencil to lightly divide a paper plate into eight equal "pie" sections. Color or paint each section a different color.
2. For the head and body, cut out a large pear shape from a brown paper bag. Glue it to the paper plate.
3. Cut out a beak and feet. Glue them in place. Draw on a wattle and other features.
4. Make a hanger by gluing a paper clip or loop of string to the back of the turkey.

Shake, Rattle, and Jump!

vitamin bottles ● rope ● uncooked macaroni ● colored tissue paper ● pompoms

1. Ask an adult to poke or cut a hole in the bottom of two vitamin bottles.
2. Starting from the bottom of the bottles, thread the ends of a 7-foot-long rope through the holes. Tie a knot at each end, then pull the rope to slide the knots into the bottles. Drop a few pieces of uncooked macaroni into each bottle, then put on the lids.
3. Glue colored tissue paper around both bottles. Let dry. Wrap clear tape around the bottles.
4. Use glue to attach pompoms onto the bottles. Let the glue dry, then shake, rattle, and jump!

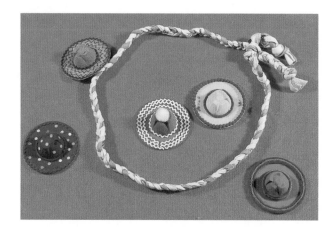

Hat Toss

lightweight cardboard ● cardboard egg carton ● decorative trims ● fabric

1. For each hat, cut one lightweight cardboard circle about 3½ inches in diameter and one cardboard egg-carton cup. Make several hats for each player.
2. Glue each cup to the center of a cardboard circle. Let dry. Decorate each hat with paint, markers, yarn, buttons, pompoms, paper-punch circles, and fabric.
3. Braid three long pieces of fabric and tie the ends together to make a ring.
4. To play, lay the ring on the floor or outside on the ground. Stand back and toss one hat at a time toward the ring. Whoever gets the most hats inside the ring wins.

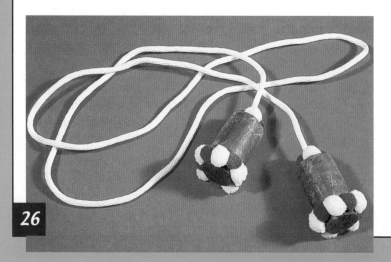

Beach Magnets

shells or other beach objects ● warm sudsy water ● small refrigerator magnets ● corrugated cardboard ● hot-glue gun

1. Collect objects from the beach, such as shells or driftwood. Scrape away any sand or dirt, and soak your items in the sudsy water.
2. Rinse the objects and let dry in the sun.
3. Lay a magnet on corrugated cardboard. Ask an adult to apply a dab of hot glue to the magnet.
4. With the help of an adult, hold one of your objects by its sides and press it down onto the glue until the glue sets. For deep shells, prepare them first by filling the curve with hot glue. This will give the magnet a flat surface to attach to. Once the glue is cooled, follow steps 3 and 4.

Butterfly Box

cardboard oatmeal container and lid ● construction paper ● stiff paper

1. Measure 1 inch up from the bottom of a cardboard oatmeal container. Ask an adult to cut off the top part, but keep the lid. Cut a hole in the center of the bottom section large enough to fit your index finger through. Paint the lid and the box inside and out.
2. Make paper flowers. Glue them inside the box, but do not cover the hole.

3. From stiff paper, cut a butterfly shape smaller than the width of the box. Decorate it. Make a paper ring to fit the tip of your index finger. Glue the butterfly to the ring.
4. Put an index finger through the hole, and put the butterfly on your fingertip. Replace the lid. Hold the box in your hands.
5. Take off the lid. Wiggle your finger to make the butterfly move.

Sleepy-Time Bear

paper ● poster board ● yarn ● felt

1. Use a 9-inch-by-12-inch piece of paper for the mattress.
2. To make a blanket, cut a 9-inch square from another piece of paper. Fold down 1 inch along one side of the paper. Turn the paper over, and put a line of glue along the other three sides of the paper. Place it over the mattress with the bottom sides even. Decorate it with cut paper or markers.
3. Cut a pillow from paper. Glue it to the top of the mattress.
4. Cut a bear shape from poster board. Color it with crayons. Tie a yarn bow around the neck.
5. Draw on a mouth. Cut eyes, eyelids, and other features from scraps of felt. Glue them in place.
6. Slide Teddy under the blanket when it's time for bed.

"Prop-er" Owl

cardboard oatmeal container ● fabric ● felt ● pebbles

1. Remove the plastic lid from a cardboard oatmeal container and cover it with fabric.
2. Cut features from felt. Glue them in place.
3. Fill the container almost to the top with pebbles. Then glue the lid in place. When dry, use the owl as a doorstop.

Sunflower Pincushion

felt ● laundry detergent bottle cap ● fabric ● plastic-foam ball ● rubber band

1. Cut flower petals from felt. Glue them around the inside edge of a laundry detergent bottle cap.
2. Cut a scrap of fabric to fit over a plastic-foam ball that is slightly larger than the opening of the cap. Gather the fabric edges under the ball, and secure them with a rubber band.
3. Glue the ball on top of the petals, with the rubber band inside the cap. Let dry.
4. Poke needles and pins into the pincushion to keep them handy.

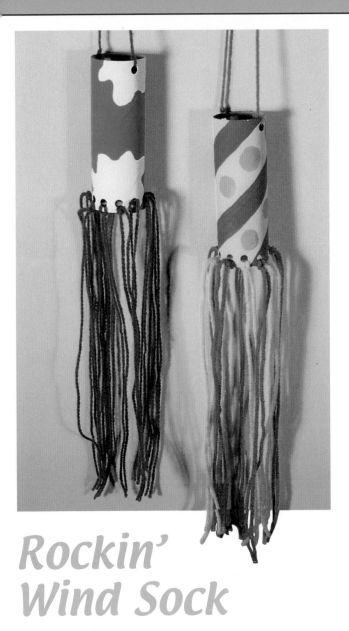

Rockin' Wind Sock

cardboard tube ● yarn

1. At one end of a short cardboard tube, punch two holes on opposite sides. This end will be the top of the wind sock. At the other end, punch holes ½ inch apart all the way around the tube.
2. Paint the tube. Let it dry.
3. For each hole in the bottom of the tube, cut a 2-foot-long piece of yarn.
4. Fold each piece of yarn in half. Thread the folded end through a hole in the bottom of the tube. Thread the ends of the yarn through the folded end and pull.
5. Cut a 2-foot-long piece of yarn as a hanger. Tie the ends to the holes in the top of the tube. Hang your wind sock outside.

Groundhog Finger Puppet

felt ● paper clip ● needle ● fishing line

1. Cut a groundhog body about 4 inches tall out of two pieces of brown felt. Cut out a belly from white felt and glue it onto one of the body shapes. Let dry.
2. Glue the front body to the back, allowing room for your finger to fit.
3. Create a snout by cutting a 1½-inch circle of felt. Snip the felt from the outside edge to the center, and then roll the circle into a cone shape. Glue the edges, hold it with a paper clip, and let dry overnight.
4. Remove the paper clip. Unbend the clip into an S shape. With a needle, thread a double thickness of fishing line through the snout. Pull the center of the fishing line behind the snout using the paper clip. Tie the fishing line so that it will stay put. Trim the "whiskers" to size. Glue the snout to a small felt circle to make the head.
5. Glue on felt eyes, nose, teeth, and ears. When dry, glue the head to the body.

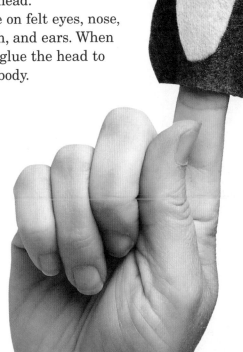

Mother's Day Bouquet

tissue paper ● chenille stick ● construction paper

1. To make each flower, cut two squares of white tissue paper, each about 4 inches by 4 inches. Decorate them with markers. Place one square on top of the other. Pinch them together in the middle, making a bow-tie shape. Wrap one end of a green chenille stick around the pinched portion. Fluff and shape the ends of the squares to look like petals.
2. Fold a sheet of construction paper in thirds. Cut out a vase shape, with the sides of the vase on the folds.
3. Tape the flower stems to the middle vase shape. Then fold in the vase on the left (to cover the stems) and glue it in place.
4. Write a message on the third vase (the inside of the card) and on the front of the card, too.

Little Brown Squirrel

cardboard tube ● construction paper ● tissue paper ● plastic egg ● thread

1. Cut a ring from a cardboard tube and paint it brown. To make the tail, draw and cut out an oval shape from brown construction paper. Use scissors to snip the edges of the oval to create furry fringe. Glue one end of the tail to the inside of the brown ring.
2. Cut small squares of brown tissue paper. Mix a little glue and water in a bowl. Use a paintbrush to spread glue over a plastic egg and apply tissue-paper squares. Brush additional glue over the tissue-paper squares. Let dry.
3. Glue the bottom of the brown egg into the ring.
4. Draw and cut little brown ears and glue on. Use a hole punch to make eyes and glue them on the head. Cut small pieces of thread for the whiskers and glue these below the eyes. Use a hole punch to make a nose and mouth. Glue in place.

"Good-bye, Teacher" Gift

craft sticks ● construction paper ● chalk ● yarn

1. Glue four craft sticks together to form a square.
2. Cut a square of black construction paper the size of the frame. Write a message in chalk on one side of the paper. On the same side of the paper, put a line of glue around the edges. Place the frame on the glue, and press in place.
3. To make a hanger, poke two holes in the top of the paper, just inside the frame. Thread yarn through the holes, and knot the ends.
4. Decorate with paper cutouts.

World's-Best-Dad Scroll

cardboard tubes ● yarn ● paper ● water ● ribbon

1. Paint two cardboard tubes. Let dry.
2. Punch a hole near each end of one tube. Tie yarn through the holes to make a hanger.
3. Cut a long rectangle from light-colored paper (slightly narrower than the length of the tubes). To make the paper look old, like parchment, run cold water on it in a sink. As it gets wet, carefully wad up the paper. Then unroll it and lay it in a dish drainer until it is completely dry.
4. Write a Father's Day message on the paper and decorate it.
5. Tape the narrow ends of the paper to each cardboard tube so that it looks like a scroll. Roll it up and tie it together with ribbon.

Snappin' Shark

cardboard tube ● paper clips

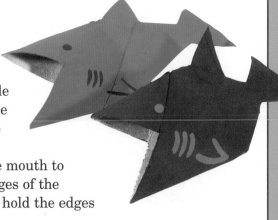

1. Flatten a short cardboard tube. At one end, cut out a triangle shape to make the shark's mouth. Save the cut pieces. At the other end, cut a triangle shape from each side of the tube to make the tail.
2. To make the dorsal fin, glue one of the extra pieces from the mouth to the opening in the tube above the tail. Glue together the edges of the shark's body and tail, but not the mouth. Use paper clips to hold the edges closed until the glue dries.
3. Paint the shark and let it dry. Draw or paint on eyes and fins. Squeeze the top and bottom of the tube to make the shark snap.

Nifty Necklace

cardboard ● cookie cutter ● yarn ● tissue paper

1. Draw a shape (such as a heart) onto cardboard, or trace around a cookie cutter. Cut out the shape.
2. Use a hole punch to make one or two holes at the top.
3. Cut a piece of yarn that is long enough to slip over your head easily when the ends are tied together. Thread the yarn through the hole or holes. Then knot the ends together.
4. Spread a layer of glue over one side of the shape. Crinkle small pieces of tissue paper into puffy balls. Press them into the glue. Let dry.

Cat Card

construction paper

1. Cut out a long heart shape from construction paper for the body. Cut out another heart for the head, two smaller hearts for the ears, and a little heart for the cat's snout.
2. Glue the ears and snout to the head. Glue the head to the pointed end of the heart body.
3. Cut two hearts for the legs and glue them to the bottom of the body. Cut out several smaller hearts. Glue these hearts to each other at the end of the body to make a tail.
4. Write "You're the Purrrrfect Valentine!" or whatever you like for your message. Add facial features with a pen.

Uncle Sam's Hat

paper ● cardboard container ● saucer

1. Glue white paper around a cardboard container.
2. Cut 1-inch-wide strips from red paper. Glue them on the container to make stripes.
3. To make the brim of the hat, trace around a saucer onto blue paper. Cut out the circle, and glue the bottom of the container on it.
4. Fill the top hat with treats.

Box-Corner Creatures

cereal box ● paper ● buttons
● feathers ● string

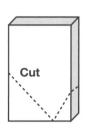

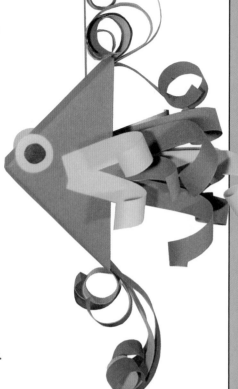

1. Cut corner sections from a cereal box, as shown.
2. Cover them with paper glued or taped in place.
3. Use one or more corner sections (taped or glued together) for each animal. Glue on features made from buttons, feathers, paper, or other materials. To make the fins on the fish, cut long strips of paper and curl them around a pencil.
4. To hang up the animal, punch two holes in the top, thread a piece of string through them, and knot the ends together.

Cut

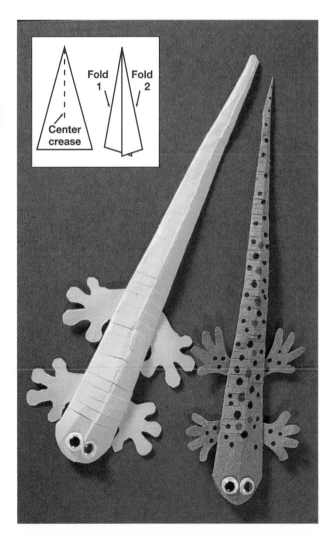

Fold 1   Fold 2

Center crease

Newt Bookmark

paper ● wiggle eyes

1. Cut a 2½-inch-by-7-inch strip of paper. Fold it in half lengthwise.
2. Cut the folded strip diagonally. Unfold the strip. The paper should form a tall triangle.
3. Fold each side of the triangle to slightly overlap the center crease, as shown in the diagram at left. Unfold.
4. Refold the triangle along the center crease. Starting an inch in from the wide end, use scissors to make snips along the folded edge. Snip only as far as the crease that is on each side. (See diagram at right.) Unfold the strip.

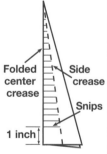

Folded center crease

Side crease

Snips

1 inch

5. Refold each side of the triangle to overlap the center crease, as in step 3. Glue the sides together where they overlap. This is the underside of the newt.
6. For the head, use scissors to round the wide end.
7. Cut out four legs from paper. Glue them to the underside of the newt. Decorate the newt with markers. Add wiggle eyes.

Fun-Shine

chenille sticks ● spring-type clothespins
● construction paper ● foam paper

1. Twirl two different-colored chenille sticks together. Twist the ends together to form a circle.
2. Paint spring-type clothespins. Let dry.
3. Clip the clothespins around the chenille-stick circle, using glue to tack into place.
4. Cut a small sunglasses shape from construction paper and glue it to the clothespins as shown. Let dry.
5. Cut out a circle of yellow or orange foam paper and glue it to the back of the clothespins.

Happy Birthday Card

construction paper ● paper towel ● yarn ● ribbon

1. Cut a piece of construction paper in half, then fold one of the halves in half to make a card.
2. To make the cake platter, cut an oval shape from construction paper and glue it to the front of the card. Cut the shape of a cake from a paper towel, and glue the cake onto the platter.
3. Cut candle and flame shapes from construction paper. Glue them to the cake. Cut pieces of yarn for icing, and glue them to the cake.
4. Use construction paper or ribbon to make a banner. Write "Happy Birthday" on it, and glue it below the cake. Write a birthday greeting inside the card.

Nutty Bugs

walnut shell ● paper ● felt ● wiggle eyes ● pompoms

1. Trace a walnut shell onto a piece of paper. Add six legs to the shape, and cut out the pattern. Trace around the pattern onto a piece of felt, and cut it out.
2. Paint the walnut shell with a few coats of poster paint.
3. Glue the shell on top of the felt legs.
4. To make the head, glue wiggle eyes onto a 1-inch pompom. Glue on a smaller pompom for a nose, then add two antennae cut from felt.
5. Glue the head to the front of the walnut shell.

Cheesy Mouse Magnet

yellow sponge ● stone ● felt ● wiggle eyes ● chenille stick ● magnetic strips

1. Cut a triangle from a yellow sponge.
2. Find a rounded stone for the mouse's body. Glue it to the sponge.
3. Glue on a nose and ears. Add eyes from felt, or use wiggle eyes.
4. For the mouse's tail, cut a 2-inch strip of chenille stick or felt. Glue one end under the back of the mouse's body.
5. Glue magnetic strips to the entire bottom of the sponge.

Tissue-Box Cover

cardboard ● felt ● masking tape

1. Cut four 5-inch-by-5¾-inch pieces from cardboard for the sides. Cut a 5-inch square of cardboard for the top.
2. In the top piece cut out a 2-inch square.
3. Using masking tape, attach the sides to form a 5-inch-square box. Add the top with masking tape.
4. Cover the entire box with felt and decorate it.
5. Slip the cover over a small box of tissues.

Eyeglasses Case

felt ● pinking shears ● chalk ● glitter ● button

1. Cut out two 4-inch-by-7½-inch pieces of felt. Use pinking shears to make a jagged edge.
2. Using chalk, write your name on one of the felt pieces. Put glue over the letters, then sprinkle glitter over the glue. Shake off the excess glitter.
3. On the second felt piece, put glue along the long edges and one of the short edges. Press the first piece on the second so that your name is on top.
4. Sew a button to the inside of the bottom piece near the opening. Snip a buttonhole in the top piece.

Magnetic Mini Memo Board

lightweight cardboard ● gift wrap ● magnetic strip ● white paper

1. Cut a 2-inch-by-4-inch piece of lightweight cardboard. Cover it with gift wrap, making a pocket at one end. Glue in place.
2. Glue a magnetic strip across the back of the memo board.
3. Cut white paper into 1½-by-2½-inch pieces and tuck them into the pocket of the memo board.
4. Hang the memo board on a refrigerator or a metal light switch to remind you of important things.

Save for a Rainy Day

plastic jar and lid ● felt ● permanent marker

1. With an adult's help, cut a slot in the plastic lid of a plastic jar, or remove the lid to add money.
2. Cut out an umbrella shape from felt, and glue it to the jar.
3. Using a permanent marker, write "rainy day fund" on the jar.
4. Add drops of glue as raindrops. Hold the jar so that the drops do not run too much.

Winter Bird

plastic half-gallon milk or juice container ● cotton balls ● star stickers ● paper ● wiggle eyes ● twig ● yarn

1. With an adult's help, cut the bottom off a plastic half-gallon milk or juice container about 1½ inches from the bottom.
2. Glue cotton balls inside the bottom piece for snow. Add star stickers.
3. Cut a bird from paper. Add a paper beak and wiggle eyes. Tape the bird to a small twig, and glue the twig across the snow.
4. Punch a hole in the top and add yarn to make a hanger.

Lacy Valentine's Day Card

construction paper
● lace or paper doily ● ribbon

1. Fold a piece of construction paper in half. Fold it in half again to form a card.
2. Glue lace or a paper doily to the front of the card, then add paper hearts and a ribbon bow.
3. Write a message inside.

Leafy Bookmark

lightweight cardboard ● construction paper ● leaves ● facial tissues ● large book ● clear self-adhesive paper

1. Cut out a 2-inch-by-6-inch piece of lightweight cardboard. Glue construction paper to both sides of the cardboard.
2. Place a few small leaves between two facial tissues. Then put the leaves between the pages of a big book to dry for a few days.
3. Glue the dried leaves to both sides of the bookmark. Glue on cut-paper eyes.
4. Cut two pieces of clear self-adhesive paper, each slightly larger than the bookmark. Remove the covering from the paper, and carefully place one piece on each side of the bookmark. Use scissors to trim the excess.

Star-Spangled Sam

striped fabric ● roll of paper towels ● felt ● ribbon ● stickers
small cardboard tube ● cotton balls ● paper ● small American flag ●
poster board ● roll of bath tissue ● chenille stick ● tinsel

1. To make the body, glue striped fabric around the bottom half of a roll of paper towels. Cut a coat from felt, and glue it around the top half. Add a ribbon bow tie and three stickers as buttons.
2. To make the head, glue a small cardboard tube on top of the body. Glue felt around it, and add cotton and cut-paper features.
3. Cut feet from paper and hands from felt. Glue them on. Put a small American flag under one of the hands. Stick the end of it under the striped fabric.
4. To make the brim of the hat, cut a large circle from poster board. Glue it on top of the head. Glue a roll of bath tissue onto the brim. Cut a circle from white paper, and glue it on top of the hat. Add stickers and a band of felt.
5. Make a sparkler by bending the end of a chenille stick around a piece of tinsel. Glue a few sparklers into the hatband.

Shadowy Fellow

paper ● craft stick ●
construction paper

1. Draw and color a groundhog on paper. Cut it out, and glue it onto one end of a craft stick.

2. Fold a piece of construction paper in half. On the fold, cut a slit for the groundhog's hole. Unfold the paper.
3. On one side of the paper, draw a sunny-day scene that shows the groundhog's shadow. On the other side, draw a cloudy-day scene.
4. Make the groundhog pop up on the sunny or the cloudy side.

Valentine-Card Buddy

cereal box ● construction paper

Heart Weave

construction paper ● yarn

1. Cut out two 3-inch-by-4½-inch rectangles from different colors of construction paper.
2. Using scissors, round off one end of each rectangle.
3. Use a pencil to lightly mark off each inch along the uncut short side of a rectangle. At each mark, make a 3-inch-long cut into the rectangle. Repeat with the other rectangle.
4. Lay the shapes flat so that they overlap and form a heart shape, as shown.
5. Weave one of the strips on the top piece under, over, then under the strips on the underneath shape. Weave the next strip over, under, then over the strips. Weave the last strip under, over, then under.
6. Tape the strips on the back of the heart to hold them in place.
7. On the front, write a Valentine's Day greeting. Punch a hole in the top, string yarn through, and give the heart to a friend.

1. On the two narrow sides and the front panel of an empty cereal box, draw a line 3 inches up from the bottom. Cut down the two corner edges of the back panel and along the line you've drawn to remove most of the sides and front. Leave the back panel whole.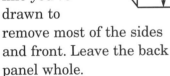
2. On the back panel, draw and cut out the shape of an animal's head and shoulders. Decorate the box with construction paper. Paint on features and details.
3. Trim and decorate the front panel to look like an animal's paws. Write your name or a valentine message on a red paper heart. Decorate it and glue it to the front.

"Chip" the Penguin

construction paper ●
black potato-chip canister and lid ●
orange foam paper ● wiggle eyes

1. Cut two wings from black construction paper. Glue them onto the sides of a black potato-chip canister.
2. Cut a long oval from white construction paper and glue it to the canister for the stomach.
3. Cut two feet and a beak from the orange foam and glue them on.
4. Glue on wiggle eyes. Let dry.

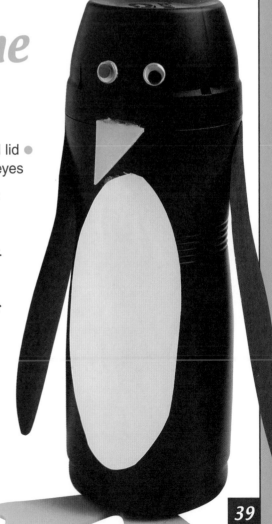

Glowing Lantern

tiny leaves ● wide-mouth glass jar ●
colored tissue paper ● small candle

1. Collect tiny leaves. Glue them around the outside of a wide-mouth glass jar, such as a salsa jar.
2. Tear colored tissue paper into small pieces. Working on one part of the jar at a time, use a paintbrush to put glue over the jar and the leaves. Lightly press the tissue-paper pieces onto the glue. Cover the entire outside of the jar.

3. Roll a piece of tape, and put it on the bottom of a small candle. Set the candle in the jar. Ask an adult to light the candle.

Safe Sparkler

thin gift-wrap ribbon ● drinking straw ● glitter

1. Cut twenty to thirty 10-inch-long strands of thin gift-wrap ribbon.
2. Holding all of the strands together, twist one end tightly. Add a few drops of glue and push the twisted end about a ½-inch into one end of a straw. Let dry.
3. For extra sparkle, dab glue onto the straw and sprinkle glitter on it.

Frog Box for Dad

cereal box ● paper ● wiggle eyes ● craft sticks

1. Cut off the top part of a cereal box so that the bottom is about 3 inches tall. Glue paper around the bottom part.
2. Tear yellow and green paper to make three flowers. Print "DAD" on them, and glue them to the front of the box.
3. Cut three frog shapes from green paper. Draw mouths with a marker, and glue on wiggle eyes.
4. Paint three craft sticks. Glue a stick to the back of each frog. Glue the sticks to the inside back of the box.

Mother's Day Envelope-Card

lightweight cardboard ● construction paper ●
old greeting cards or gift wrap ● fabric

1. Cut out a 7-inch-by-10-inch piece of lightweight cardboard and a 7-inch-by-11-inch piece of construction paper.

2. Glue the cardboard onto the construction paper so that the extra inch of paper sticks out on the right-hand side. Fold the cardboard in half, leaving the 1-inch flap sticking out on the right.

3. Decorate the inside and outside of the card with paper, pictures from old greeting cards or gift wrap, and markers. Add a message.

4. Close the card, and fold the 1-inch flap over the top part. Cut a 1-inch-by-2-foot piece of fabric, and tie it around the card to hold it closed.

Foam Animal

plastic-foam tray ● paper or fabric ● yarn
● needle

1. On each curved end of a plastic-foam tray, bottom-side up, draw an animal's body with legs, as shown. In the center of the tray, draw a head with a neck. Cut out the pieces.

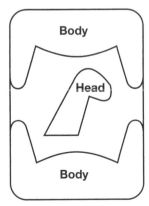

Body

Head

Body

2. Decorate the pieces, and add features with crayons, cut paper, or fabric.

3. Place the head between the two body pieces, and carefully sew them together at the top with yarn. Leave the rest open so the animal can stand up.

Earth Day Magnet

cardboard ● blue and green yarn
● ribbon ● magnetic strip

1. Cut a circle from cardboard.
2. Lightly pencil in the shapes of the earth's continents.
3. Apply a thin layer of glue to the cardboard. Press short strands of green and blue yarn into the glue. Use blue for the oceans and green for land. Fill in all the spaces. Let dry.
4. Glue ribbon around the rim of your cardboard earth, leaving the ends loose. When the glue dries, tie the ends in a bow.
5. Glue a magnetic strip to the back. Give your magnet to a friend on Earth Day, or keep it as a reminder to take care of our earth.

Puppy Pals

sandpaper ● felt ● pompom ● wiggle eyes ● safety pin ● foam paper ● ribbon

1. Draw a dog-biscuit shape on sandpaper. Cut it out. Cut out ear shapes from felt. Glue them onto the sandpaper biscuit. Add a pompom as a nose and wiggle eyes.
2. To make a pin, glue a safety pin to the back of a sandpaper dog.
3. To make a bracelet, cut out a 1-inch-by-7-inch piece of foam paper. Punch a hole at both ends, and tie on a ribbon at one end. Glue a sandpaper dog to the center of the foam bracelet.
4. To make a necklace, glue three sandpaper dogs onto a 2½-foot-long piece of ribbon. Let the glue dry.

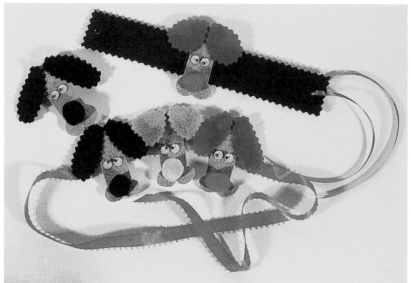

Secret Heart

construction paper ● white bond paper

1. Cut a heart from red construction paper.
2. Draw a flower with six petals on white bond paper, and cut it out. Use crayons or colored pencils to decorate the petals and to write a secret message in the center. Fold each petal inward, covering the message.
3. Turn the flower over, add a few dots of glue, and press it onto the heart.
4. On the back of the heart write "Float this heart in water, and watch a message bloom." When the heart is placed in a bowl of water, the petals will slowly open and your message will be revealed.

Rich Critters

cardboard tube ● corrugated cardboard ● yarn
● wiggle eyes

1. Cut a coin slot in the side of a cardboard tube.
2. On corrugated cardboard, draw an animal's body and legs, as shown, two times. Cut out the shapes. Glue one shape on each end of the tube.
3. Cut a head and neck from cardboard. Glue them on.
4. Paint the bank. Add yarn details and wiggle eyes.
To remove money from your bank, break open the tube.

Plane Game

poster board ● paper plate ● stickers ● yarn
● spring-type clothespin

1. For the airport, cut out a 10-inch square from poster board. Draw a circle on it by tracing around a small paper plate. Cut out the circle. Decorate the airport with markers and stickers.
2. Punch a hole in two corners of the airport. For a hanger, tie yarn through the holes.
3. For the airplane, use markers to color a spring-type clothespin.
4. From poster board, cut out one long oval shape for the wings and two short ones for the tail. Add stickers. Glue the wing shape into the "mouth" of the clothespin. Glue the "mouth" closed. Glue on the tail shapes.
5. Hang the airport in a tree or another place outside. Place a twig on the ground a few feet away from the airport, and stand behind it. Take aim, and toss the plane through the hole in the airport. Invite friends to play.

Tooth-Pillow Pal

felt ● yarn ● stuffing material

1. Cut two large matching tooth shapes from white felt.
2. Cut features and arms from felt. Glue the features to one tooth shape and the arms to the underside of it.
3. Position this tooth shape on top of the other. Use a hole punch to make holes around the shapes, about ½ inch in from the edges.
4. Tightly wrap tape around the end of a long piece of yarn (to make it like the end of a shoelace). Lace the yarn through the holes around the sides and bottom of the shapes, leaving the top open.
5. Stuff the pillow with batting, cotton balls, or other stuffing material. Do not overstuff.
6. Finish sewing the top. Knot the ends of the yarn together.

Tote Bag

cereal box ● gift wrap ● fabric trim ● poster board ● metal fasteners

1. Tape an empty cereal box closed.
2. Turn the box so that a long narrow side is facing you. Cut a line down the center of this side from top to bottom. Cut the top and bottom edges so the two halves of the side will fold into the box. Tape them in place.
3. Cover the box with gift wrap, and decorate it with fabric trim.
4. Cut out and decorate two strips of poster board for handles. Punch a hole in each end of the strips, then punch two holes in each side of the box. Use metal fasteners to attach the handles to the insides of the box. Tape the fasteners in place.

Handle Racer

plastic-bag handle ● poster board ● paper clips ● small cup ● metal fasteners

1. Cut off the hard-plastic handle from a plastic bag.
2. Cut out two identical car-body shapes from poster board. Glue them together with the bottom of the handle between them. Hold them in place with paper clips until the glue dries.
3. Trace around the bottom of a small cup four times onto poster board. Cut out the circles, then punch a hole in the center of each.
4. Punch two holes in the car. Place one wheel on both sides of each hole. Attach the wheels with a metal fastener (loosely, so that the wheels can spin).
5. Use markers to decorate the car.

Fluttering Ladybug

paper plate ● black and red paper ● metal fasteners ● wiggle eyes

1. Cut the edges of a paper plate to look like flower petals. Color the center of the flower.
2. Cut out an oval from black paper. Trace around it onto red paper. Cut out the red oval.

3. For the body, glue the black oval to the flower. To make wings, cut the red oval in half lengthwise. Fold down one end of each half.
4. Add spots to the wings with markers. Punch a hole in the folded section of each wing. Poke matching holes in the body (and plate) with a ballpoint pen. Attach the wings to the body with metal fasteners.
5. Draw legs and glue on wiggle eyes.

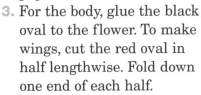

Erasable Teddy Bear

black construction paper ● cardboard ● yarn ● chalk ● felt ● ribbon

1. Draw a teddy-bear shape on black construction paper, and cut it out. Glue it to cardboard. Let dry. Trim the cardboard around the bear.
2. Use a paintbrush to spread white glue over the entire teddy bear. Let it dry.
3. Punch a hole in each ear, and tie yarn through for a hanger. Punch a hole in one paw, tie yarn through it, and tie a piece of chalk to the other end.
4. Cut features from felt, and glue them on the bear. Tie a ribbon bow around its neck.
5. Write messages on the bear with chalk. Use a dry cloth to erase them.

Chenille-Stick Penguin

black and white chenille sticks ● orange foam paper ● wiggle eyes

1. Bend a black and a white chenille stick in half. Put the two together, black over white.
2. Twist the chenille sticks once at the top about an inch from the fold to form the head. Bend each black end up to form wings, and wrap the excess around the neck.
3. Twist the ends of the white chenille stick together, leaving about an inch at the bottom. Bend each end out.
4. Cut two feet and a beak from orange foam paper. Glue the feet to the ends of the white chenille sticks.
5. Glue on the beak and wiggle eyes. Let dry.

Patriotic Wind Sock

pushpin ● white film canister ● red and white ribbon ●
blue and white electrical tape ● fishing line

1. Use a pushpin to punch two holes in the bottom of a white film canister.
2. Cut three red and three white streamers from ribbon, each about 6 inches long. Tape them around the canister.
3. Starting at the bottom, wrap blue electrical tape around the canister and ribbons, overlapping each row.
4. Cut squares of white electrical tape. Then cut each square in half to make two triangles. Press the triangles onto the blue tape as shown to make a five-point star.
5. Thread the ends of a long fishing line through the two holes in the bottom of the canister and tie a knot to secure it. With your parents' permission, attach the wind sock to the family car's antenna or on the porch or in a breezy window.

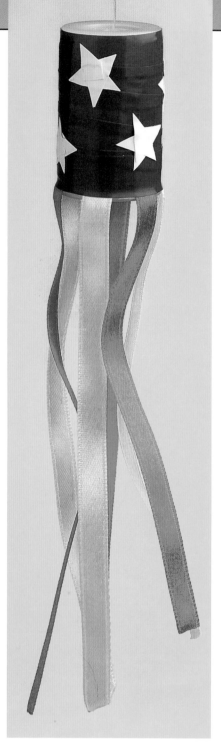

Niña, Pinta, or Santa María

paper ● cereal box ● drinking straws

1. On paper, draw a side view of a ship small enough to fit on the side of a large cereal box. Cut this out as a pattern.

2. Trace around the pattern on both large sides of the cereal box, using one of the long, narrow sides as the bottom of the ship. Cut out the ship. Turn it inside out so that the inside of the box forms the outside of the ship.
3. Paint the outside of the ship, or glue on cut paper.
4. Cut a sail from white paper. Decorate it if you like. Punch a hole in the top and bottom of the sail.
5. Place the end of one drinking straw into the end of another to make a mast. Slide the mast through the holes. To hold the sail in place, put a piece of transparent tape onto the mast above and below where the mast and the sail meet.
6. Glue or staple the top edges of the ship together, with the mast inserted between them.

Bead Rings

twist tie ● tiny beads

1. Peel the paper or plastic covering from a twist tie.
2. Bend one end of the wire so the beads won't fall off. Push the other end through the centers of tiny beads.
3. When the wire is almost covered, test the length by wrapping it around your finger, then remove the ring.
4. Twist the wire ends together. Ask an adult to help you trim the wire ends with scissors and push them in so they won't scratch your finger or hand. You may want to wrap a small piece of tape around the wire ends.

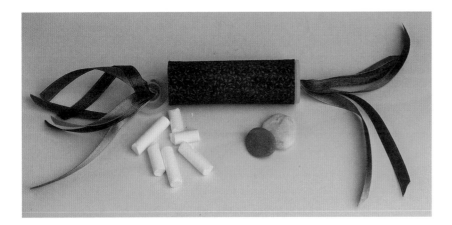

Hopscotch-to-Go

packing tape ● two film canisters ● masking tape ● fabric ● ribbon ● paper clip ● chalk ● pebbles

1. Use packing tape to attach two film canisters end-to-end.
2. Run a strip of masking tape around the rim of each canister.
3. Cut a piece of fabric about 4½ inches by 5½ inches. Fold the fabric under at the edges, and then glue it around the canisters.
4. Poke holes in each canister's lid. Cut three strands of ribbon and fold them together in half. Open the paper clip and use it as a threading tool to pull the center of the ribbons through one of the holes. Knot the ribbon so that it stays put. Do the same for the other canister lid.
5. Fill one canister with chalk to draw the hopscotch grid and the other end with pebbles to use as markers.

Shamrock Pin

green poster board ●
pinking shears ● paper doily ●
green paper ● ribbon ● safety pin

1. Cut out a circle from green poster board. Use pinking shears for a zigzag edge.
2. Cut out a smaller circle from a paper doily.
3. Draw and cut out a shamrock from green paper.
4. Tie some ribbon into a bow.
5. Glue everything together. Let it dry.
6. Glue a safety pin to the back.

Wacky Creature

old magazines

1. Look through old magazines and, with an adult's permission, cut out pictures of different parts of people, animals, and objects.
2. Arrange the pictures on paper to create a wacky new creature. Glue the pictures in place.

Remembering Beads

key-chain ring ● beading cord ● seven beads

1. Tie a key-chain ring securely in the middle of a 25-inch beading cord.
2. Thread one end of the cord through a bead. Thread the other end of the cord through the other side of the same bead. Pull.
3. Continue adding beads as in step 2, pulling the cord tight after each one. Keep the beads aligned and the cord evenly spaced.
4. Tie the cord ends together about an inch from the last bead. Trim the ends, then knot them or leave them plain. Apply a dab of glue to the cut ends so they don't fray.
5. Remembering Beads help remind us to treat others with respect, tolerance, courtesy, love, kindness, courage, and humility. When you do something that reflects one of the messages above, slide a bead along the cord.

Fabric Father's Day Card

paper ● fabric

1. To form the card, fold a piece of paper in half.
2. Draw shapes or letters on fabric scraps. Cut them out and arrange them on the front of the card. Glue them on and let dry.
3. Use markers to add details, if you wish. Write a message inside.

Tube Racer

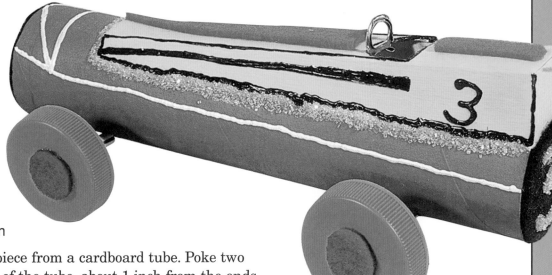

cardboard tube ●
lightweight cardboard
● cardboard box ●
corrugated cardboard
● plastic jug caps ●
drinking straws ●
tab from a soft-drink can

1. Cut an 8-inch-long piece from a cardboard tube. Poke two holes near each end of the tube, about 1 inch from the ends.
2. Trace each end of the tube onto lightweight cardboard. Cut out the circles. Glue them to the ends of the tube. Let dry.
3. Cut off one side of a narrow cardboard box (such as a toothpaste box) at an angle. Cut a hole in it to make the driver's seat. Glue it to the side of the cardboard tube opposite the holes. Let dry. Then paint the car.
4. Cut two circles from corrugated cardboard to fit inside a plastic jug cap. With a hole punch, make a hole in the center of each circle. Glue the two cardboard circles together, then glue them inside the cap. Let dry. Repeat with three more caps to make four wheels.
5. To make axles, cut two 4-inch-long pieces from drinking straws. Insert the axles through the holes in the tube. Glue the ends of the axles into the holes of the wheels.
6. Decorate the car. Use a tab from a soft-drink can to make the windshield.

Windowsill Planter

plastic tubs ● fabric ● pebbles ● soil ● plant

1. Find two plastic tubs that are the same size.
2. Set a tub on the less colorful side of a large piece of fabric. Trace around it onto the fabric. Measure the height of the tub and add 2 inches to that. Enlarge the circle by that amount on all sides.
3. Cut out the large circle. Set the tub in the center. Fold the edges of the fabric up and into the tub.
4. Place the other tub into the fabric-covered tub. Staple the sides of the tubs together.
5. Put pebbles in the bottom of the planter for drainage. Add soil and a plant.

Secret Valentine

white construction paper ● watercolor paint

1. Cut out a heart from white construction paper. Use a white crayon to decorate it with designs and a message. Press hard.
2. On the back, use a pen to write: "Brush the other side with watercolors pink to find a secret message in invisible ink!"
3. Give the valentine to a friend. When he or she paints the other side, the message will be revealed.

Corny Cutouts

yellow and green paper ● pompoms ● chenille stick ● twine ● magnetic strips

1. Cut out two ear-of-corn shapes from yellow paper. Cut out two cornhusk shapes from green paper. Glue the husks on the ears.
2. For corn kernels, glue on pompoms.
3. For stalks, tape a green chenille stick to the back of each ear of corn. Tie them together with twine.
4. Hang them on a door or in a window, or glue magnetic strips to the back and put them on a refrigerator.

Rainbow-Tailed Comet Ball

ribbon ● small plastic-foam ball ● large paper clip

1. Cut different-color ribbons to 18-inch lengths.
2. Use a pencil to push a hole through the plastic-foam ball.
3. Unbend the paper clip to its S shape. Use the clip as a threading tool by pushing it through the ball and grabbing the ribbons together at their center point. Pull the clip and ribbons through to the opposite end of the ball. Discard the paper clip.
4. Push the ribbons aside and fill the area around it with glue. Let dry.
5. Play catch with your comet ball, or mount it on a stick and whirl it through the air.

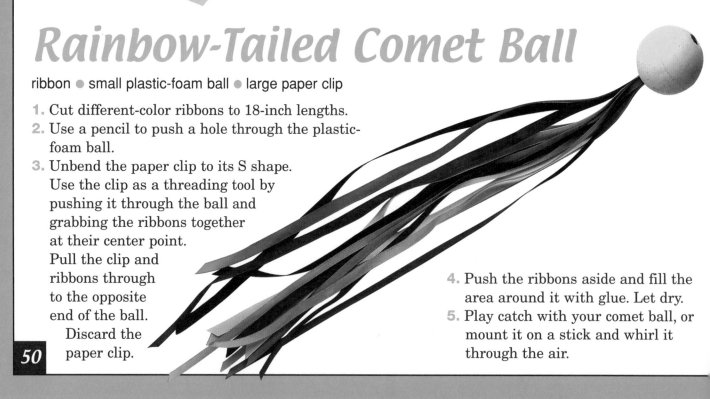

Fragrant Decoration

corrugated cardboard ● cinnamon sticks ● spices ● dried beans ● seeds ● whole cloves ● dried orange-rind pieces ● yarn

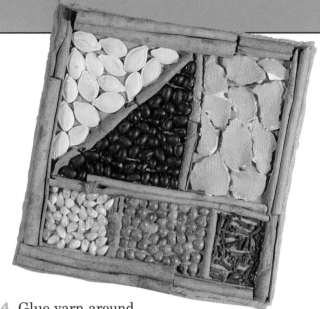

1. Cut a 6-inch square from corrugated cardboard.
2. Ask an adult to help you break or cut cinnamon sticks to glue around the edges of your decoration. Glue on small pieces to divide the middle into sections.
3. Spread glue inside each section, and arrange spices, dried beans, and seeds on the glue. Whole cloves and dried orange-rind pieces add a nice scent.
4. Glue yarn around the edge of the plaque. For a hanger, tape or glue a piece of yarn to the back. Hang the plaque in your kitchen, or give it as a gift.

Frog Mouse Cover

paper ● felt

1. Trace around your computer mouse onto a piece of paper. Add 2 inches all around the tracing and add flipper-feet to the sides to create a frog pattern.
2. With a marker, trace around your pattern twice onto a piece of green felt. Cut out both pieces. Cut out a tongue from red felt.
3. With the tongue in between, glue the two pieces together around the edges, leaving the back open. Let dry. Decorate the frog.
4. Slip the frog over your computer mouse when you're not using it to keep away the dust.

Seashore Sun Catchers

chenille stick ● thread ● tissue paper ● glitter ● paper

1. Bend a chenille stick into the shape of a sea creature. Tie a thread loop to the top for a hanger.
2. Cut a piece of tissue paper so that it's slightly larger than the shape. Glue it onto the shape, keeping the thread loop out of the way. Let dry.
3. Trim the excess paper from around the edge of the shape.
4. Decorate the sea creature by gluing on glitter or bits of chenille stick or paper.
5. Hang your sun catcher in a window.

Triple-Treat Valentine

paper ● small box ● thin ribbon
● wrapped candies

1. Use paper to decorate a small box.
2. Cut a 4-foot length of thin ribbon. Tie on a wrapped piece of candy every 6 inches.
3. From paper, make a small heart and a card to fit in the box. Write "Pull me" on the heart. Decorate the card and add a message.
4. Glue the card to one end of the candy rope. Glue the heart to the other. Let the glue dry.
5. Put the card in the box, and place the candy rope on top of it. Roll a piece of tape, and use it to attach the heart to the inside top of the box, as shown. Close the box.
6. When your valentine opens the box, he or she will pull the heart for a triple surprise: a candy rope, a card, and a pretty box.

Fish Sticks

craft sticks ● wiggle eyes ● yarn

1. Paint ten craft sticks, and let them dry.
2. Arrange the craft sticks as shown. Glue them in place. Let dry.
3. Glue a stick along the center of the shape on both sides. Add wiggle eyes. Let the glue dry.
4. For a hanger, tie a piece of yarn through the fish. If you wish, make several fish and create a mobile.

Pie-Pan Art

pie tin ● corrugated cardboard ● fabric ribbon

1. With a pencil, draw a simple design on a pie tin.
2. Place the tin on a piece of corrugated cardboard. Use a ballpoint pen to poke holes along the pencil lines.
3. Cut a piece of fabric ribbon to fit around the edge of the tin. Glue in place.
4. Glue on a ribbon loop as a hanger.

Leaf and Flower Press

craft sticks ● corrugated cardboard ● paper towels
● two rubber bands

1. Lay two craft sticks on a table, parallel to each other and 1¾ inches apart. Run a ribbon of glue along the center of each craft stick, stopping ½ inch from each end.
2. Lay nine craft sticks close together across the two sticks with glue. Wipe away any excess glue.
3. Repeat steps 1 and 2 to make the other side of the press. Allow both sides to dry. Paint both sides of the press.
4. Cut pieces of corrugated cardboard and paper towel to fit between your leaf press. To use the press, lay a leaf or flower between two pieces of paper towel and sandwich the paper towel pieces between two sections of cardboard. Repeat to include up to six flowers or leaves.
5. Keep the press tight with two crisscrossed rubber bands.
6. Check the press after several days to see if the leaves are thoroughly dry.

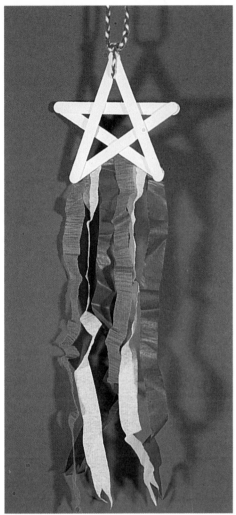

Wind Star

craft sticks ● yarn ●
crepe or tissue paper

1. Glue five craft sticks into a star shape as shown. Let dry.
2. Paint the star, or color it with markers.
3. To make a hanger, braid three strands of yarn and tie the braided yarn to the star.
4. Cut six strips from crepe or tissue paper. Glue them along the bottom of the star.
5. Hang the wind star where it can catch a breeze but won't get rained on.

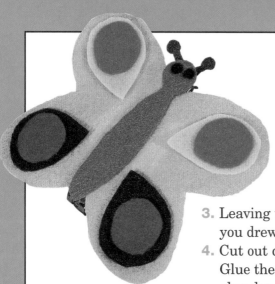

Butterfly Barrette

flat barrette ● felt

1. Select a flat barrette.
2. Fold a piece of felt in half. Starting at the fold, draw half of a butterfly. The length of your butterfly along the fold should be at least as long as the barrette.
3. Leaving the felt folded, cut along the line you drew. Open the butterfly.
4. Cut out details from felt. Glue them in place. Let the glue dry.

5. Open the barrette, and glue the butterfly on top of it. Cut out a square of felt, and glue it to the underside of the barrette, as shown.

Rockin' Horse

cardboard tube ● craft sticks ● cardboard oatmeal container ● lightweight cardboard ● felt ● yarn

1. Poke two slits, about 1 inch apart, near each end of a short cardboard tube. Push one end of a craft stick into each hole to make the horse's legs. Glue them in place and let dry.
2. To make the rockers, draw three pencil lines, each 1 inch apart, around a cardboard oatmeal container. Cut down the side and along each pencil line, then cut the three curved strips in half.
3. On four of the strips, use a hole punch to make two holes about 2½ inches from either end. Push a craft stick through each hole to make the holes a bit bigger. Line up the holes in two of the strips. Glue these strips together. Then glue them onto one of the strips with no holes. Do the same with the other strips.
4. Position the bottom of the horse's legs in the holes. Glue them in place. Let dry.
5. Cut a horse's head and two ears from lightweight cardboard. Glue the ears to the head. Cut a slit about 1½ inches long in one end of the body, on the top. Slide the head into the slit and glue it in place.
6. Paint the horse and rockers. Cut eyes and a saddle from felt. Use yarn to make a mane and bridle. Glue in place.
7. To make the tail, cut several 3-inch-long pieces of yarn. Tie them together near one end with another piece of yarn. Glue that end inside the back of the cardboard tube. Glue scraps of cardboard inside the back of the body if it needs balancing.

Gator Clip

spring-type clothespin ●
lightweight cardboard ● wiggle eyes ● magnetic strip

1. Paint a spring-type clothespin green. Paint the "teeth" of the clip part white.
2. Cut three small connected triangles from lightweight cardboard. Paint them green, and let dry. Glue them on the alligator's back. Glue on wiggle eyes.
3. Use your alligator as a paper clip or as a snack-bag clip. Or glue a magnetic strip on the bottom and hang the alligator clip on the refrigerator to hold messages.

Earth Toss

heavy cardboard ●
blue and green yarn

1. Cut a 3-inch-by-4-inch piece of heavy cardboard. Wrap alternating bands of blue and green yarn around the cardboard to create a pompom. Each band should be wrapped about fifty times.
2. Slip the pompom off the cardboard and tie it tightly around the middle. Snip the loops and fluff. Trim as needed to create a round earth shape.
3. To play, gather several friends in a circle and toss the earth. For fun, pick geography categories such as countries, oceans, states, or cities. See if you can name one example in your category each time the earth ball comes to you.

Puffy Bracelet

flexible plastic container ● sandpaper ● pompoms or tissue paper

1. With an adult's help, cut a circular band from a flexible plastic container, such as a shampoo bottle. Cut the band, breaking the circle, and round the ends. Use sandpaper to smooth any rough edges.
2. Glue pompoms or crumpled tissue-paper balls around the band. Let the glue dry.

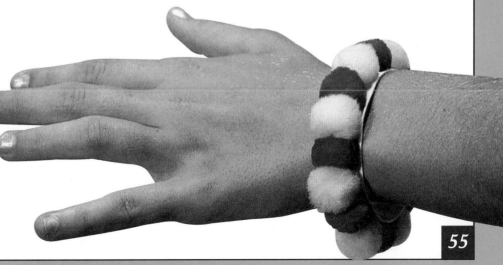

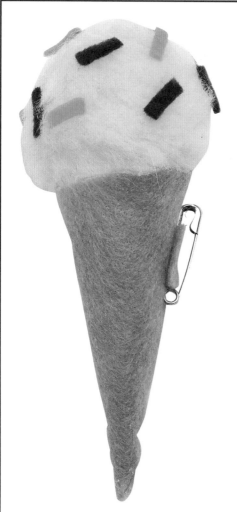

Boat Float

plastic foam trays ● paper ● toothpicks ● wooden spool ● wooden bead ● felt

1. From a plastic-foam tray, cut out a shape for the base of the boat.
2. For the cabin, cut out three rectangles and two squares from another tray. (The sides of the squares should be as long as the short ends of the rectangles.) Cut windows in two of the rectangles.
3. Assemble and glue the cabin onto the base. Make a chair from plastic-foam pieces, and glue it onto the base.
4. Create flags from paper, and glue them onto toothpicks. Stick the flags into the top corners of the cabin.
5. Make a toy person using a wooden spool, a wooden bead, and felt. Glue the person onto the chair.

Bug Bracelets

felt ● pinking shears ● artificial leaves ● pompoms ● paper ● Velcro ● needle and thread

1. Cut out three 1-inch-by-7-inch strips of felt. Use pinking shears to create zigzag edges.
2. Cut out three leaf shapes from green felt, or use three artificial leaves. Use pompoms, felt, and punched-paper circles to create a ladybug, a caterpillar, and a butterfly. Glue a bug on each leaf. Let dry.
3. Use glue to attach pieces of Velcro to the ends of the strips so that you can clasp them around your wrist. Glue a piece of Velcro on the back of each leaf and in the middle of each strip so that you can attach each bug to a bracelet. Let the glue dry.
4. For fun, switch the bugs on the bracelets whenever you like, or trade bugs with friends.

Ice-Cream-Cone Pin

felt ● cotton balls ● 2-inch pompom ● safety pin

1. Make a cone about 3 inches long from brown felt, and stuff it with cotton balls.
2. Glue a 2-inch pompom on top of the cone, and add candy or chocolate chips cut from felt.
3. Glue a safety pin onto the back, and glue a small piece of brown felt over the glued side of the pin to make it more secure.

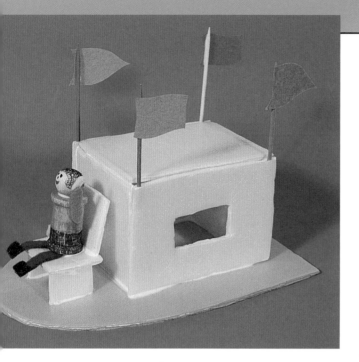

Plate of Lobster

paper plate ● metal fasteners ● construction paper ● wiggle eyes

1. Use crayons to color the front and back of a paper plate.
2. See diagram for this step. Cut the plate into three sections. Cut two triangles out of one end of the middle section. Cut one triangle out of one end of each side section. Punch holes, as shown.
3. Use metal fasteners to attach the side sections (claws) onto the middle section (body).
4. Cut out legs from the scrap triangles, and make antennae from construction paper. Glue them onto the body. Add wiggle eyes.

Clay Picture

cardboard ● water ● clay

1. Cut a piece of cardboard any shape you'd like.
2. Mix about a tablespoon of white glue with a few drops of water. Knead together the glue with a handful of clay.
3. Press the clay against the cardboard and flatten it out.
4. Add glue and water to other colors of clay in the same way, and press these colors into your design.
5. Add texture to the clay by using your fingertips, the back of a spoon, the tines of a fork, or a marble.
6. When your design is done, coat it with a thin layer of glue mixed with a few drops of water.

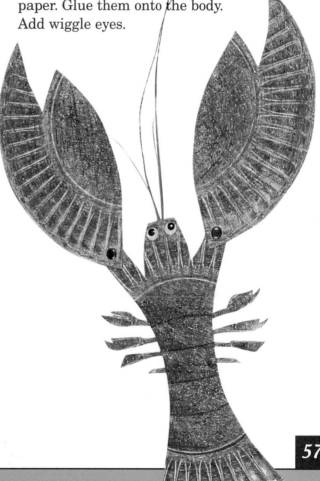

Independence Hall

half-gallon and half-pint milk cartons ● shoebox ●
red, white, and blue paper
● small white paper cup

1. Tape down the top of a half-gallon milk carton.
2. Cover the carton and the shoebox with red paper. For the roofs, cover the top of each with blue paper. Glue the carton onto the front of the shoebox.
3. Tape down the top of a half-pint milk carton, and cover it with white paper. Glue it on the steeple base. Decorate a small white paper cup, and glue it upside down on top of the carton. Form a cone shape from a paper triangle, and glue it on top.
4. From paper, cut out windows, doors, and a clock. Add details with markers, and glue the shapes on the building.

Colorful Turkey

brown paper ● paper

1. Fold a piece of brown paper in half. Draw a line across it 1 inch up from the fold. Draw a turkey resting on the line. Keeping the paper folded, cut along the line, around the turkey, then back along the line.
2. Unfold the paper. Fold up just the turkey on each side (not the bottom inch). Glue the heads together, then glue the tops of the bodies together. On the base, fold the crease inward to form a stand, as shown.
3. Cut out two wings from paper. Use crayons to add details. Glue just the front part of each onto the turkey. Bend the ends out a little.
4. From paper, cut out a head shape, an eye, a beak, and a wattle for each side. Glue them on.
5. Cut out four tail feathers of varying sizes, and fold them in half. Cut four slits in the tail and insert the feathers, with the smallest in front.

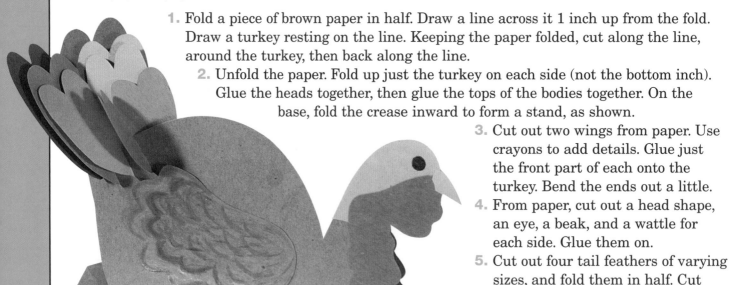

Coaster Set

cardboard ● clear self-adhesive paper ● fabric ● 1-gallon water jugs ● felt ● yarn ● soup box

1. Cut out a 3½-inch-wide circle from cardboard for a pattern.
2. Cut a piece of clear self-adhesive paper to measure 8 inches wide and 12 inches long, and stick it on an 8-inch-by-12-inch piece of fabric.
3. Using the cardboard pattern, trace and cut out six circles from the sides of a water jug, six circles from the felt, and six circles from the fabric-adhesive paper combination.
4. Glue the coasters together in the following order: fabric on top, plastic from the jugs in the middle, and felt on the bottom. Then glue yarn around the edge of each coaster.
5. Cut an inch off the top of a soup box and cut a section from the front, as shown.
6. Cover the box with felt, decorate it, and store your coasters in it.

Felt Snake Puppet

felt ● fabric

1. Cut out two rectangles from blue felt and one from red felt. Each should be about 2 inches longer and wider than your hand (with your fingers together).
2. Fold the red rectangle in half. Round the corners. Using it as a pattern, round the corners on one end of each blue rectangle.
3. Refold the red rectangle in half. Place one blue rectangle on top of it and the other beneath it, lining up all the rounded edges. Glue these edges in place.
4. Glue the sides of the blue rectangles together, leaving the end open.
5. Cut out features from felt and fabric. Glue in place.

Zooming Airplane

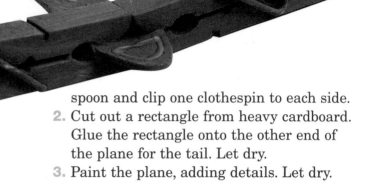

wooden ice-cream spoon ●
two spring-type clothespins
● heavy cardboard

1. Dab some glue on the larger end of a wooden ice-cream spoon and clip one clothespin to each side.
2. Cut out a rectangle from heavy cardboard. Glue the rectangle onto the other end of the plane for the tail. Let dry.
3. Paint the plane, adding details. Let dry.

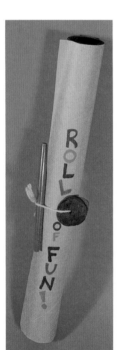

Fun Roll

paper grocery bag ● yarn ● pen

1. Cut along the side of a paper grocery bag, then cut off the bottom to form a long strip of paper.
2. On the strip, use markers to draw a checkerboard, a maze, a dot-to-dot activity, tic-tac-toe boards, and a picture for coloring.
3. From the bag bottom, cut out twenty-four circles for checkers. Color twelve red and twelve black. Punch a hole in the center of each. String them onto a long piece of yarn.
4. Roll up the strip and tie it with the yarn. Write "Roll of Fun!" on the outside. Tuck a pen under the yarn.

Window Card

construction paper ●
photo or fabric ● ribbon

1. To form a card, fold a piece of construction paper in half, then fold it in half again. Use a pencil to mark the front.
2. Unfold the card. On the front section, draw a simple design and cut it out to form a window.

Bottled "Sand" Art

clear plastic bottle and lid ● colored chalk ● sandpaper ● bowls ●
measuring cup ● salt ● funnel or paper coffee filter ● ribbon

1. Soak off the label from a clear plastic bottle.
2. To make colored "sand," grind a half-stick of colored chalk against sandpaper into a bowl. Mix in ¼ cup of salt. Make several colors, each in its own bowl. The total amount should be enough to fill the bottle.
3. Spoon layers of colored "sand" through a funnel into the bottle. (To make a funnel, poke a hole in a paper coffee filter.)
4. Use a blunt pencil to push designs into the layers.
5. Put the lid on the bottle, and add a ribbon, if you wish. (*Do not use the salt on food after mixing it with chalk.*)

Magical Map

poster board ● metal paper clip ● strong magnet ● ruler

1. On poster board, draw and color a bus and a map of a town. (The bus should be able to fit on the roads that you draw.)
2. Cut out the bus, and glue a metal paper clip on the back. Place it on the map.
3. Glue a strong magnet on the end of a ruler. Hold it under the map where the bus is. As you move the magnet, the bus will move with it. "Drive" the bus around town.
4. If you wish, create trains, people, animals, and other movable objects. Glue a paper clip on the back of each, and move them around, too. Give a magnet to a friend and play together.

3. Trim a photo or a piece of fabric so that it's slightly larger than the window. Glue or tape it behind the window.
4. Remake the first fold of the card, and glue those two sections together.
5. Remake the second fold. Punch holes along the top and bottom of the front section, and weave ribbon through them.
6. Write a message inside.

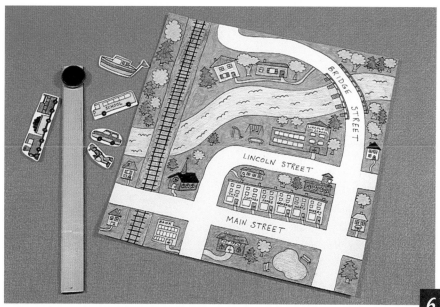

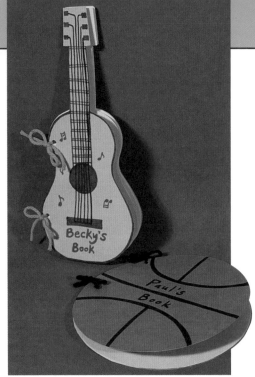

Cool Address Book

poster board ● paper ● yarn

1. For your book, select a simple shape that's special to you, such as a basketball or a guitar. Draw the shape on poster board and cut it out.
2. Trace around the shape once onto poster board and eight times onto paper. Cut out the shapes.
3. Place the paper shapes between the two poster-board shapes. Punch two holes at the edge of each shape, and tie all of them together with two pieces of yarn.
4. Decorate the cover of your address book. Inside, write the names, addresses, e-mail addresses, phone numbers, and birthdays of people you know. Or leave the book empty and give it as a gift.

Year-Round Fireflies

square tissue box ● felt ● chenille stick ● pompoms ● wiggle eyes ● aluminum foil ● thread ● plastic wrap

1. Cut "windows" from the sides of a square tissue box, leaving about ¾ inch on each edge.
2. Turn the box so that the tissue opening is on the bottom. Glue on a piece of felt to fit over what is now the top of the box. Using scissors, make two holes in the top and poke a chenille stick through them. Bend the ends to secure them.
3. Glue two small pompoms together to make each bug. Add wiggle eyes and a tiny pompom on one end to make a face. Crunch up a small piece of aluminum foil to make the "lighted" tail. Add felt wings.
4. Tie thread around each bug. Tape each thread to the roof.
5. From plastic wrap, cut four pieces to fit the windows, then glue them to the edges inside the box. (The easiest way to do this is to use a glue stick or a cotton swab dipped in glue.)

Father's Day Box

shoebox with lid ● paper

1. Separately cover a shoebox and lid with paper.
2. Cut out shapes from various colors of paper. Cut out letters if you wish to put a name on the box. Use a hole punch to make small circles.
3. Arrange and glue the shapes on the lid of the box to form a "mosaic" design.
4. Give the box to your dad so that he can fill it with CDs or golf balls and tees, fishing lures, or anything he likes.

Napkin Gobblers

cardboard tube ● felt ● craft feathers ● wiggle eyes

1. Cut a cardboard tube into 1-inch rings. Make one ring for each dinner guest.
2. Cut strips of felt, and glue one to each cardboard ring. Before the glue dries, slip two or three craft feathers between the felt and the cardboard.
3. From felt, cut out a peanut shape for each turkey's head, a small diamond shape for its beak, and a curvy shape for its wattle. Glue the shapes together. Add wiggle eyes.
4. Glue a turkey head to each ring.

Neon Bracelet Holder

cardboard ● felt ● small cardboard tube

1. Cut out a 5-inch square from cardboard for the base and cover it with felt.
2. Cut out a cardboard circle to cover the top of a cardboard tube. Glue it in place.
3. Cover the tube with felt, decorate it, and glue it to the base.
4. Add trim to the base.

Index